[redacted]

[redacted]

BEGINNING CALCULATOR MATH

Gerardus Vervoort • Dale J. Mason

A FEARON MAKEMASTER® BOOK

Fearon Teacher Aids
Carthage, Illinois

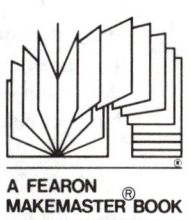

[redacted]

The Calculator Math Series:

Beginning Calculator Math (Book 1)
Intermediate Calculator Math (Book 2)
Advanced Calculator Math (Book 3)

Consultant: Alan Ovson
Cover designer: Susan True
Editorial and graphic services: Sheridan Publications Services, Nevada City, California

Note: Beginning Calculator Math, Intermediate Calculator Math, and *Advanced Calculator Math* are based on *Calculator Activities for the Classroom 1, 2, and 3* (ditto master books), and *Calculator Activities for the Classroom: Teacher's Resource Book*, published by Copp Clark Publishing, a division of Copp Clark Limited, Toronto, Canada. Some additional activity sheets may be found in the original publications, which are available from Copp Clark Publishing, 517 Wellington Street West, Toronto, Ontario, Canada, M5V 1G1.

ISBN-0-8224-1200-4

Printed in the United States of America.

Preface

I have always endeavoured according to my strength and the measure of my ability to do away with the difficulty and tediousness of calculations, the irksomeness of which is wont to deter very many from the study of mathematics.

John Napier
From the *Dedication of Rabdologiae*

This comment by the inventor of logarithms still applies today. Manipulation of numbers is not the prime objective of an arithmetic program—in fact, it is only a minor part. People must know *when* to multiply and subtract as well as know *how* to multiply and subtract. They also must know what information is required to solve a problem and whether a proposed answer is reasonable.

Problem solving in the broadest sense is the essence of mathematics, and it is here that we find the calculator's value to the mathematics program. With the calculator eliminating the drudgery of lengthy calculations, the student can concentrate on the problem-solving process. Here are some specific situations where the calculator is useful:

– Estimating—mentally grasping the overall proportions of an operation—is an essential skill. The calculator enables students to make estimates and then rapidly get feedback on their correctness. Interestingly, while the calculator facilitates development of estimating skills, using a calculator also increases the need for that ability, for minor operating slips or use of a calculator with a low battery can easily produce incorrect answers. Users must thus develop a feeling for what the answer to a problem should be, and critically examine the answers that are displayed. *Elementary Calculator Math, Intermediate Calculator Math,* and *Advanced Calculator Math* each contains a series of activities to improve the students' ability to find approximate answers to addition, subtraction, multiplication, and division problems. Note that many educators differentiate between *estimation* and *approximation*, and the distinction may be useful. We have chosen to use the term *estimation* to cover both meanings. Those wishing to help their students learn both terms are encouraged to do so.

– Problem solving using mathematics is enhanced by use of the calculator. Students (and others) have often been dissuaded from attacking some types of problems because of the length of the computations involved. The calculator frees them to concentrate on what information is required to solve a problem, what steps and operations are involved, and what answers are reasonable. The *Intermediate* and *Advanced* books, in particular, show how both everyday problems and more intricate mathematical ones (too cumbersome for paper and pencil solution) can be handled easily with the aid of the calculator.

- Understanding of fractions can be enhanced by use of the calculator. It can also be used to develop the concept of a fraction and the relationship between common and decimal fractions. Calculator algorithms can be developed for operations with fractions. It should be noted that in spite of emphasis on the metric system and the increased emphasis on decimal fractions, common fractions have not disappeared entirely (nor should they). Not only is the concept of 1/3 much easier to grasp than $0.\overline{3}$, but students in the intermediate grades must be prepared to deal with algebra of the form $\frac{a+b}{c}$. Also, fractions provide opportunities for students to think their way through various calculator algorithms. The *Intermediate* and *Advanced* books contain many activities that use common and decimal fractions. A series of exercises is included to help students perform operations such as 3/4 + 5/8 on the calculator.
- Detecting and identifying patterns is the essence of inductive reasoning. The calculator can be the "number laboratory" where the student performs a series of numerical experiments, develops a hypothesis, and checks the conclusion by further experiments. In the past, these types of exercises, though recognized as desirable, were impossible due to the drudgery of the required computations. Many activities on patterns in all three *Calculator Math* books provide opportunities for students and teachers to engage in this type of experimentation.
- All teachers know that games, tricks, and puzzles help motivate students. They can be used to drill facts, expand concepts, and provide opportunities for discovery. Therefore, each book of *Calculator Math* contains a section of games and similar activities for individuals, small groups, or whole classes.

The *Calculator Math* books have been created to make connections between the calculator's capabilities, the learning of concepts in mathematics, and the application of those concepts and the calculator's capabilities to realistic problems. The flexible MAKEMASTER® duplicatable format enables any of the activity sheets to be used in multiple copies with minimal expense. The teacher's guide and skill-and-topic annotations on the activity sheets help connect the activities to the mathematics curriculum. Many of the activities suggested on the sheets can be continued with similar material provided by the teacher or invented by the students. We urge teachers to go further than we have, to build even more activities for their classes. They will enrich their mathematics program by doing so; they will help their students productively use one of the technological marvels of the twentieth century; and they will mightily please Mr. Napier's ghost besides!

The Authors

Note: Materials and literature on calculator applications in the mathematics program are rapidly proliferating. Readers who wish to pursue the subject in greater depth are advised to write the Calculator Information Center, 1200 Chambers Road, Columbus, Ohio 43212 (Telephone 614-422-8509). The center publishes a regular bulletin, free of charge, listing available materials and other resources.

Contents

1-26 The Hidden Message 36
· *Estimating in multiplication*

1-27 Whiz Quiz 37
· *Estimating in multiplication*
· *Rounding to the nearest ten or hundred*

1-28 Quick Parts 38
· *Estimating fractional parts*

1-29 The Educated Guess: Part I 39
· *Estimating in division*

1-30 The Educated Guess: Part II 40
· *Estimating in division*

1-31 The Line-Up 41
· *Estimating in division*
· *Rounding to the nearest whole number*

Eleven Activity Sheets with Games

1-32 Checking the Facts 42
· *Reviewing addition facts*

1-33 The Nimble-Minded Adder 43
· *Reviewing addition facts*
· *Detecting patterns*
· *Developing strategies*

1-34 The Nimble-Minded Subtractor 44
· *Reviewing subtraction facts*
· *Reviewing multiplication facts*
· *Detecting patterns*
· *Developing strategies*

1-35 The Nimble-Minded Multiplier 45
· *Reviewing multiplication facts*
· *Reviewing division facts*
· *Detecting patterns*
· *Developing strategies*

1-36 The Nimble-Minded Divider 46
· *Developing factoring skills*
· *Reviewing division facts*
· *Detecting patterns*
· *Developing strategies*

1-37 Mental Magic 47
· *Reviewing number facts*

1-38 Operation "Close Watch" 48
· *Reviewing number facts*
· *Developing strategies*

1-39 Three-Button Blues 49
· *Reviewing number facts*
· *Developing strategies*

1-40 Dangerous Division 50
· *Reinforcing division skills*

1-41 Big Number Wins 51
· *Understanding order of operations*
· *Using special calculator algorithms*

1-42 The Magician 52
· *Developing algebraic reasoning*

Two Activity Sheets on Patterns

1-43 Pattern Mysteries: Part I 53
· *Detecting and extending patterns*

1-44 Pattern Mysteries: Part II 54
· *Detecting and extending patterns*

Eight Activity Sheets on Problem Solving

1-45 The High Cost of Crime 55
· *Solving problems*
· *Organizing data*

1-46 Some Costs of Living 56
· *Increasing consumer awareness*
· *Solving problems*

1-47 Going Camping 57
· *Increasing consumer awareness*
· *Constructing tables*

1-48 Traveling in North America 58
· *Estimating in addition*
· *Reading maps*

1-49 The Great Carpet Sale 59
· *Increasing consumer awareness*
· *Finding area*
· *Finding price per unit*

1-50 Painting the Shed 60
· *Finding area*
· *Developing consumer skills*

1-51 MacDonald's Fence: Part I 61
· *Calculating area and ratio*

1-52 MacDonald's Fence: Part II 62
· *Calculating area and ratio*

Answer Key 63

Activities Overview

Activity Category:	Beginning Calculator Math	Intermediate Calculator Math	Advanced Calculator Math
	Activity sheet numbers in:		
Learning About the Calculator	1–10	1–8	1–5
Estimation	11–31	9–20	6–9
Games	32–42	21–28	10–15
Fractions		29–32	16–20
Patterns	43–44	33–34	21–30
Problem Solving	45–52	35–43	31–43
Content Lessons		44–47	44–46

Note: For ease of reference and to avoid the implications that *Beginning, Intermediate,* and *Advanced* may have for students, the teacher's notes and MAKEMASTER® activity sheets in the three *Calculator Math* books carry a double number. The first number indicates the book (*1-* denotes sheets in the *Beginning* book, *2-* sheets in the *Intermediate* book, and *3-* sheets in the *Advanced* book). The second number gives the activity-sheet number within that book. Thus, *2-14* indicates activity sheet 14 in the *Intermediate* book.

Topics-and-Skills Overview

Topics/Skills	Beginning Calculator Math (Book 1) Sheet numbers	Intermediate Calculator Math (Book 2) Sheet numbers	Advanced Calculator Math (Book 3) Sheet numbers
Calculator Mechanics			
familiarization with the calculator	1, 2, 3, 4, 5, 6, 7, 8, 10		1, 2, 3
speed and accuracy with the calculator	2, 3, 4, 5, 6, 7, 8, 10		
optimum use of the calculator		1, 2, 3, 4, 5, 6, 8	1, 2, 3, 4, 5, 18, 19 20, 35
judicious use of the calculator	9		32
special calculator algorithms	41		18, 19, 20, 44, 45, 46
Whole Numbers			
addition facts	2, 6, 7, 8, 10, 32, 37 38, 39	22	
subtraction facts	3, 6, 7, 8, 10, 33, 37 38, 39		
multiplication facts	4, 6, 7, 8, 10, 37, 38 39	1, 24, 26	10, 11
division facts	5, 6, 7, 8, 10, 37, 38 39, 40	24	10
order of operations	41	1, 8	
Estimation			
rounding	11, 12, 13, 14, 15, 16, 17–27, 28–31	10–21	6, 8, 9
estimation, addition	11, 12, 13, 14, 15, 16 48	9, 10, 11, 35	6
estimation, subtraction	17, 18, 19, 20, 34		6, 14
estimation, multiplication	21–27, 34, 35	12–19, 23, 25, 26, 36, 37, 41, 42	7, 8, 11, 13, 14
estimation, division	29, 30, 31, 35, 36	20, 21, 26	9, 11
large numbers		43	41, 42
using estimation to solve equations		45, 46	

Topics/Skills	Beginning Calculator Math (Book 1) Sheet numbers	Intermediate Calculator Math (Book 2) Sheet numbers	Advanced Calculator Math (Book 3) Sheet numbers
Common/Decimal Fractions			
concepts		29, 44	
equivalent fractions		29, 30, 31, 32	16, 17
converting, fractions/ decimals		29, 30, 31, 32	16, 17
operations with fractions	28		18, 19, 20
Problems			
using intuition		33, 34	
developing strategies	32, 33, 34, 35, 36, 38 39		42
developing mathematical reasoning			30, 44, 45, 46
solving problems	45, 46, 47, 49, 51, 52	35, 36, 37, 38, 39, 40, 41, 42, 43	4, 5, 15
Patterns			
detecting/completing	33, 34, 35, 36, 43, 44	23, 33, 34, 44	21, 22, 23, 24, 25, 26, 27, 28, 29, 30
explaining		44	22, 23, 24, 25, 26, 27
Handling Data			
reading/constructing tables, graphs, diagrams	14, 47, 48	39, 40	31, 35, 36, 37
gathering/organizing data	45, 46	35, 37, 41, 42, 47	12, 15, 31, 34, 36, 37, 39
data and averages		22, 41, 42	12, 33, 34, 36, 37
Rate, Ratio, Percent			
rate, ratio, percent	49, 50, 51, 52	38, 41, 42	32, 34, 35, 36, 37, 38, 39, 40, 42
interest			1, 2, 4, 5
taxation			3, 31
consumer awareness	45, 46, 47, 49, 50	35, 36, 37, 38	1, 2, 3, 4, 5, 31, 32, 36

Topics/Skills	Beginning Calculator Math (Book 1) Sheet numbers	Intermediate Calculator Math (Book 2) Sheet numbers	Advanced Calculator Math (Book 3) Sheet numbers
Measurement			
linear measurement	49–52	38–42	
volume		38, 39, 41, 42	
area	49, 50, 51, 52	39, 40	
time		43	
Other Concepts			
number properties		5, 6, 7, 8, 44	18, 25, 26, 27
factors/multiples	36	24	10, 15
exponents, squares/square roots		4, 25	14, 22, 23, 24
limits			7, 28, 29, 39
pi		39, 47	40
negative integers		2	6
developing algebraic reasoning	42	27, 28, 45, 46	25, 26, 27, 43
inverse operations			44, 45, 46
significant digits	31	44	

Teacher's Guide

NOTE: Some Recommendations for Calculator Purchases

To many people, a calculator is a calculator. However, there are great differences between different brands and models of calculators. These differences include the type of logic employed, which dictates the order in which keys must be struck. Other differences are: available functions (%, $\sqrt{\quad}$, and so on); size of display; automatic/manual constant; floating/fixed decimal point; automatic display shut-off; size; spacing and arrangement of keys; sturdiness of case; durability; and power source.

Selection of a particular model depends on the grade levels of the students who will be using the machine, and on the purposes of the program. Features that seem mandatory for calculators intended for intermediate school students include: sturdiness; algebraic mode (natural order arithmetic); floating decimal point; 8-digit display; automatic constant.

Rechargeable batteries are (or were) a frequent cause of breakdown. Moreover, depending on the recharging mechanism, the constant connection of rundown units to an external power source can be a nuisance. On the other hand, replacement batteries can be very costly in the long run.

Due to the large number of variations among calculators, it is most desirable that all students in the elementary classroom use the same model.

*Ten Activity Sheets for Learning About the Calculator**

1-1 Keys to the Calculator's Heart

Focus on . . .

- *Introducing the calculator*

Notes

1. If possible, arrange to have one calculator for each student. However, two, or even three students per calculator is easily workable.
2. Be aware that some of the students may have had previous experience with a calculator. The investigation phase can vary from a few minutes to half an hour, depending on the needs of the students.
3. The students will need some "tinker time" to satisfy their natural curiousity about the calculator. This tinker time is easily blended into their introduction to work with the activity sheets.
4. If students bring their own calculators, make sure that the calculators operate in the algebraic mode so they are compatible with the handouts.

Extension

After the students have become acquainted with the calculators and have finished the activity sheet, play some number fact games with them. Have them use the calculators to find such numbers as:

$$3 + 5 + 8 + 9 + 3 - 7 - 11 = ?$$

or

$$4 \times 5 \times 6 - 14 \times 2 \div 6 = ?$$

1-2 The Speeding Addition Problem

Focus on . . .

- *Learning the calculator keys*
- *Practicing addition facts*

Notes

1. Adjust the time for this sheet as required. Three minutes may be too short for many groups.
2. Check the answers with your class and discuss how groups of problems on this sheet (and their answers) are related.

*For solutions, see *Answer Key*, pp. 64–68.

Extensions

1. You may want to make up similar problem sheets to give the students additional practice.
2. Your students may use the sheet both with the calculator for help in familiarization with the calculator keys, and without the calculator, for reinforcing addition facts. Students can time each other to decide whether they can work the problems faster with the calculator or without it.

1-3 The Speeding Subtraction Problem

Focus on . . .

- *Learning the calculator keys*
- *Practicing subtraction facts*

Notes

1. See *Notes* for sheet 1-2.
2. Discuss the relation between addition and subtraction, pointing out that $7 - 2 = 5$ because $5 + 2 = 7$.

Extensions

1. See *Extensions* for sheet 1-2.
2. Have students make up word problems using the numbers from the subtraction problems.

1-4 The Speeding Multiplication Facts

Focus on . . .

- *Learning the calculator keys*
- *Practicing multiplication facts*

Notes

1. See *Notes* for sheet 1-2.
2. Using an example such as $3 \times 4 = 12$ and $4 \times 3 = 12$, point out that the order isn't important when numbers are multiplied (i.e., multiplication is *commutative*).

Extensions

1. See *Extensions* for sheet 1-2.
2. Ask students to decide whether addition and subtraction are commutative. They should give examples to support their conclusions.

1-5 The Speeding Division Facts

Focus on . . .

- *Learning the calculator keys*
- *Practicing division facts*

Notes

1. See *Notes* for sheet 1-2.
2. Discuss the relation between multiplication and division, pointing out that $12 \div 3 = 4$ because $4 \times 3 = 12$.

Extensions

1. See *Extensions* for sheet 1-2.
2. Have students explore what happens when zeros are added to the dividend and the divisor. Give them the following problems and have them draw a conclusion: $63 \div 7$, $630 \div 7$, $630 \div 70$, $6300 \div 7$, $6300 \div 70$, $6300 \div 700$.

1-6 The Great Mathematical Message

Focus on . . .

- *Learning the calculator keys*
- *Practicing calculator operation*

Extension

Have students try to write messages of their own by making up problems and using the codes shown.

1-7 Monster Math

Focus on . . .

- *Practicing calculator operation*

Note

Students may have difficulty with Problem 26. Explain that $14^2 = 14 \times 14$ and that 14^2 is read "fourteen squared." Emphasize that any number multiplied by itself can be written using this shorthand notation.

Extension

Ask some students to prepare similar exercises for their classmates.

1-8 Crossnumber Puzzle

Focus on . . .

- *Developing speed and accuracy*

Extension

Almost any similar material may be used. Some students can be assigned the task of making up crossnumber puzzles.

1-9 Calculator versus Calculator

Focus on . . .

- *Using the calculator judiciously*

Notes

1. This exercise provides the opportunity for the students to see that at times, they can "outthink" the calculator.
2. Use a clock with a prominent second hand or call out the time every 15 seconds. Make sure that all the students start at the same time.
3. In many cases, the students should beat the calculator. Discuss why this occurs.

1-10 The Great Turnover

Focus on . . .

- *Working with large numbers*
- *Developing speed and accuracy*

Notes

1. While the fact that certain combinations of numerals resemble words is essentially trivial, it can be used from time to time to check accuracy. Students can become very intrigued by the results. Check that students know how to translate certain words by turning their calculators upside down.
2. For 34 Across, explain that $2^3 = 2 \times 2 \times 2$ and is read "two cubed."

Extension

Challenge students to make up number sentences whose answers can be inverted and read as words.

*Twenty-one Activity Sheets on Estimation**

1-11 Bigger Number Tips the Scales

Focus on . . .

- *Estimating in addition*
- *Rounding to the nearest ten*
- *Comparing sizes of numbers*

Notes

1. Students will need to know how to round 3-digit numbers to the nearest ten.
2. While students may be tempted to calculate the first answer exactly, the relative simplicity of estimating will probably lead them into estimation long before the page is finished. Since mental addition of multiples of 10 and 100 may be difficult for many students, they should write down the rounded sum before attempting comparison.
3. The third pair of numbers (109 + 72 and 90 + 90) may cause initial difficulty for some students. Encourage them to examine the results of their rounding. Point out that when 109 is rounded to 110, 1 is added; when 72 is rounded to 70, 2 is subtracted. Thus, the rounded sum, 110 + 70, is 1 less than the exact sum, 109 + 72.

1-12 Which is Greater?

Focus on . . .

- *Estimating in addition*
- *Rounding to the nearest ten or hundred*
- *Comparing number values*

Note

This is an extension of the preceding sheet. Discuss with students the methods they used to find the answers. In most cases, they should round both sums before comparing. If the sums are equal when they round to hundreds, they should check by rounding to tens.

1-13 One Higher, One Lower

Focus on . . .

- *Estimating in addition*
- *Rounding to the nearest ten*

Notes

1. This exercise is designed to help the students decide whether the exact answer will be somewhat more or somewhat less than the answer obtained from rounding.
2. Discuss the relation between the three sums in a triangle, pointing out that the top sum in each triangle has been rounded two different ways to form the two bottom sums. Discuss how the rounding influences the sum.

Extension

Some students may be interested in different methods of rounding. Discuss the odd-even method and the five-or-more-round-up method. Ask students to consider the advantages and disadvantages of each method.

1-14 Guess the Shortest Route

Focus on . . .

- *Estimating in addition*
- *Rounding*
- *Reading maps*

*For solutions, see *Answer Key*, pp. 69–79.

Note

Make sure students estimate first, then calculate.

Extension

Have students draw various maps of your area showing several surrounding towns and the distances between them. Then challenge them to write problems similar to the ones on this sheet.

1-15 How Many Hundreds: Part I

1-16 How Many Hundreds: Part II

Focus on . . .

- *Estimating in addition*
- *Rounding to the nearest hundred*
- *Adding four-digit numbers*

Note

Have the students put away their calculators and estimate first the number of hundreds in each problem. Most students should not find it necessary to write down the rounded numbers before finding the sum. Explain that for estimation to be useful, it should be a quick mental process. After they are finished with the page, have them work out the exact answers with or without their calculators.

1-17 About the Same

Focus on . . .

- *Estimating in subtraction*
- *Rounding to the nearest ten*
- *Subtracting three-digit numbers*

Note

Have the students follow this process:

1. Round the numbers in the left-hand column.
2. Find the numbers in the right-hand column that are similar to those in the left-hand column.
3. Join the two with a line.
4. Circle the larger pair of numbers.

1-18 Speedy Subtraction: Part I

1-19 Speedy Subtraction: Part II

Focus on . . .

- *Estimating in subtraction*
- *Rounding to the nearest ten or hundred*

Note

Have the students estimate first. Their estimated answers will probably vary. Discuss why this is so and whether it is more effective to round to the nearest ten or to the nearest hundred. Point out that to be useful, estimation must be both fast and reasonably accurate. After they finish estimating, they may calculate the exact answers with or without the calculator.

1-20 Find the Smaller Number

Focus on . . .

- *Estimating in subtraction*
- *Comparing subtraction sentences*
- *Adjusting for rounding error*

Note

After students complete this sheet, discuss the effects of rounding either the first or second part of the subtraction sentence. Ask students to give examples from the sheet to illustrate different cases.

1-21 Round and Multiply

Focus on . . .

- *Estimating in multiplication*
- *Rounding to the nearest ten*
- *Multiplying rounded numbers*

Notes

1. Exercises like this activity sheet may be supplemented with oral or flash card exercises.
2. Students should realize that if they round *down* to the nearest ten, the exact answer will be *larger* than the estimate. If they round *up*, the exact answer will be *smaller*.

1-22 Easy Multiplication

Focus on . . .

- *Estimating in multiplication*
- *Rounding to the nearest ten or hundred*

Note

Make sure that students do the estimate first, then work the problem. In this way, they will learn from mistakes and improve on subsequent estimates.

1-23 Guess One Higher, One Lower

Focus on . . .

- *Estimating in multiplication*
- *Rounding to the nearest ten*

Notes

1. This exercise helps students understand that estimates enable them to determine the range of a multiplication product. Have the students estimate the P> (product greater than) and P< (product less than) before calculating the exact answer.
2. After students have completed the sheet, ask how they can tell which end of the range the exact product will be closer to.
3. Discuss how to reduce the range of the products, encouraging the students to examine their estimated products. You may want to present the idea of adding 10 to the lower estimate and subtracting 10 from the upper estimate. Help students decide when this does not work (in a problem such as 61 X 8) and why.

1-24 Code Puzzle

Focus on . . .

- *Estimating in multiplication*
- *Rounding to the nearest ten or hundred*

Note

Have the students round the factors and estimate the products for all the code letters first. Then they should find the box whose range will include the product. If two estimated products have the same range, have them use their calculators to find the exact products.

Extension

Have students make up code puzzles such as the ones on this sheet. They can include addition and subtraction as well as multiplication problems.

1-25 Number Line Puzzle

Focus on . . .

- *Estimating in multiplication*
- *Adjusting for rounding error*
- *Using a number line*

Note

Ask students to be as careful as possible in putting the letters on the number line; some of the answers are very close together. Have them round the factors and estimate all the products first. If two of the estimated products are the same, they should look again at the factors to determine the order of the products. Encourage students to determine the order without using their calculators to find exact products.

1-26 The Hidden Message

Focus on . . .

- *Estimating in multiplication*

Note

Again, have students estimate all the products first. They should determine the order from the factors if two estimated products are the same.

1-27 Whiz Quiz

Focus on . . .

- *Estimating in multiplication*
- *Rounding to the nearest ten or hundred*

Note

Some teachers prefer that the student indicate an awareness that the "real" answer is somewhat more or less than the estimate by putting "+" or "–" after the estimate. The exact answers are given. As with all estimation problems, estimates from the students will vary.

Extension

Give students some problems with three or more factors. Discuss the methods they could use to estimate the products.

1-28 Quick Parts

Focus on . . .

- *Estimating fractional parts*

Notes

1. Some students may need to be reminded that to find 1/3 of a number you divide by three. Then ask them how they would find 2/3 of a number.
2. The estimated answers are likely to vary greatly because students will use different methods for determining divisibility.

1-29 The Educated Guess: Part I
1-30 The Educated Guess: Part II

Focus on . . .

- *Estimating in division*

Note

This sheet provides an opportunity to introduce the concept of significant digits. Students can find the quotients to one or two significant digits instead of finding exact quotients.

1-31 The Line-Up

Focus on . . .

- *Estimating in division*
- *Rounding to the nearest whole number*

Notes

1. The letters placed correctly do not spell words as on previous activity sheets.
2. Have students use a "+" or "–" as shown in the example to indicate whether the exact quotient is more or less than their estimate.
3. Students should know how to round tenths to the nearest whole number.

Eleven Activity Sheets with Games

1-32 Checking the Facts

Focus on . . .

- *Reviewing addition facts*

Notes

1. To make it easier to play this game, glue the game board onto a sheet of heavy paper before cutting out the minicards.
2. Provide a pair of scissors for every two students and an envelope in which they may store the minicards.

Extensions

1. This game provides a good opportunity to teach or review the concept of tally marks.
2. Similar minicards can be made to review subtraction, multiplication, and division facts.

1-33 The Nimble-Minded Adder

Focus on . . .

- *Reviewing addition facts*
- *Detecting patterns*
- *Developing strategies*

Notes

1. Suggest that students write the target number.
2. Give the students an opportunity to play several games before asking them to develop a strategy.
3. A common target for the whole class will aid in the discovery of a strategy. Start with 38.
4. It should be discovered that with the target 38, whoever gets to 28 first will be the winner. It usually takes repeated experiences before the students realize that whoever gets to 18 first will get to 28 first and then therefore to 38 first.
5. Finally, the students realize that the first player should punch in 8.

Extensions

Use the same target numbers, 25–50.

1. Have the students play the game using the numbers 1 through 5. With target number 38, the winning strategy is 2, 8, 14, 20, 26, 32, 38.
2. Have the students play the game using the numbers 1 through 14. With target number 38, the winning strategy is 8, 23, 38.
3. Have the students play the game using the numbers 3 through 9. With target number 38, the winning strategy is 14, 26, 38.

1-34 The Nimble-Minded Subtractor

Focus on . . .

- *Reviewing subtraction facts*
- *Reviewing multiplication facts*
- *Detecting patterns*
- *Developing strategies*

Notes

1. Allow several games to be played before asking students to develop a strategy.
2. A common target for the whole class will aid in the discovery of a strategy. Start with 43.
3. Students will discover that the multiples of 10 are the winning positions, for example, the sequence 40, 30, 20, 10.

Extensions

Use the same target numbers 25–50.

1. Have the students play the game using the numbers 1 through 8. The winning strategy is the sequence of multiples of 9. (For target number 43: 36, 27, 18, 9.)
2. Have the students play the game using the numbers 4 through 12. The winning sequence is the multiples of 16. (For target number 43: 32, 16.)
3. There are many variations to this game: Vary the target number from 0 to another number. Apply other restrictions to the choice of numbers. For example, use numbers 1 through 9 except 7, or no two odd numbers in a row. The games that can be made up are unlimited.

1-35 The Nimble-Minded Multiplier

Focus on . . .

- *Reviewing multiplication facts*
- *Reviewing division facts*
- *Detecting patterns*
- *Developing strategies*

Notes

1. The strategy for this game is parallel to the Nimble-Minded Adder, but is more difficult to see at first. Make certain the class has mastered that game before introducing this one.
2. Allow several games to be played before asking for a strategy.
3. To aid in discovering a strategy, have all students use the same target, 144.
4. The winning strategy consists in reaching a number between 72 and 144. This in turn depends on who reaches $72 \div (2 \times 9) = 4$ first.

Extension

This game can be simplified if necessary by restricting the options to pressing 2, 3, or 6. Strategy for 144 is the sequence 72, 6.

1-36 The Nimble-Minded Divider

Focus on . . .

- *Developing factoring skills*
- *Reviewing division facts*
- *Detecting patterns*
- *Developing strategies*

Notes

1. The strategy for this game is similar to the Nimble-Minded Subtractor but much more difficult. Make certain that the students understand the preceding games before introducing this one.
2. Allow several games to be played before pressing for a strategy.
3. To aid in discovering and discussing the strategy, have all students start with the same number, 144.
4. The winning strategy consists of leaving the opponent with a number which has no divisors between 2 and 9, for example, 1 or numbers such as 121, 127, and so on.

Extension

The game can be simplified at first by using only 2 and 4 as allowable divisors. This can then be extended to allowing only 2, 4, and 8, or only 2, 3, and 6.

1-37 Mental Magic

Focus on . . .

- *Reviewing number facts*

Note

Instead of using the paper flap taped over the calculator display, some teachers prefer to use a wide rubber band. The decision may depend on the model of calculator the students are using.

1-38 Operation "Close Watch"

Focus on . . .

- *Reviewing number facts*
- *Developing strategies*

Notes

1. Insist that the students keep a written record of the answers that appear in the display. It avoids arguments about whether or not an answer has been displayed earlier, and aids in remembering the number facts.
2. For the first few games, students should use one-digit operator and target numbers.

1-39 Three-Button Blues

Focus on . . .

- *Reviewing number facts*
- *Developing strategies*

Notes

1. Scores are improved if students are restricted to only one or two operations at first. Avoid division, except in the higher grades. Students should discover that certain numbers such as 18 have very few combinations; others, such as 8, have many more.
2. To avoid arguments, you may suggest that the first student write down which three buttons are going to be used.

1-40 Dangerous Division

Focus on . . .

- *Reinforcing division skills*

Notes

1. Before the students cut out the number cards, have them paste their copy of the sheet on heavier paper. Have scissors available to cut out the number cards.
2. After students have played the game for awhile, review some of the divisibility rules.

1-41 Big Number Wins

Focus on . . .

- *Understanding order of operations*
- *Using special calculator algorithms*

Notes

1. Review order of operations using "Please My Dear Aunt Sally" (Parentheses, Multiplication, Division, Addition, Subtraction).
2. Review division by zero.

1-42 The Magician

Focus on . . .

- *Developing algebraic reasoning*

Notes

1. Be sure students understand what it means to *square* a number.
2. Review the use of boxes, circles, triangles for unknowns, or use variables if students are familiar with them.
3. After playing the age trick, summarize by developing the equality:

$$[(10 \times \square + 10) \times 10] + \Delta - 100 = 100 \times \square + \Delta$$

4. After playing the chain trick, you may want to consolidate the learning by translating it into the equality:

$$(\square + 1)^2 = \square^2 + 2 \times \square + 1$$

pointing out that

$$\begin{aligned}(\square + 1)^2 &= (\square + 1) \times (\square + 1) \\ &= (\square + 1) \times \square + (\square + 1) \times 1 \\ &= \square^2 + \square + \square + 1 \\ &= \square^2 + 2 \times \square + 1\end{aligned}$$

This concept may be difficult for some students.

*Two Activity Sheets on Patterns**

1-43 Pattern Mysteries: Part I

Focus on . . .

- *Detecting and extending patterns*

Note

Make sure that the students guess *before* checking with the calculator

Extension

Ask students to find methods for checking 66,666 × 66,667 = 4,444,422,222 on their calculators.

*For solutions, see *Answer Key*, pp. 80–83.

1-44 Pattern Mysteries: Part II

Focus on . . .

- *Detecting and extending patterns*

Extension

Students may want to construct similar patterns for their classmates.

*Eight Activity Sheets on Problem Solving**

1-45 The High Cost of Crime

Focus on . . .

- *Solving problems*
- *Organizing data*

Extension

Advertisements and catalogs can be used to supplement this exercise.

1-46 Some Costs of Living

Focus on . . .

- *Increasing consumer awareness*
- *Solving problems*

Note

Emphasize the importance in estimating when shopping for a number of items.

Extensions

1. This exercise can generate a discussion about food and about what food is consumed daily in students' own households.
2. Students can make lists of items to buy and can shop for these items in newspaper advertisements. They will have to keep a complete list of their purchases and costs.

1-47 Going Camping

Focus on . . .

- *Increasing consumer awareness*
- *Constructing tables*

Note

Discuss what might be needed on a two-week camping trip.

Extension

Bring several sporting goods catalogs to class and have students compare the prices for the same item (such as a sleeping bag). Use this as the basis for a discussion of developing wise shopping practices. Be sure to bring out that the quality of an item should be weighed against its price.

1-48 Traveling in North America

Focus on . . .

- *Estimating in addition*
- *Reading maps*

Extension

Have students locate several other cities on the map. Then have them find out the distances to some of the cities shown. They can also write problems similar to those on the sheet.

1-49 The Great Carpet Sale

Focus on . . .

- *Increasing consumer awareness*
- *Finding area*
- *Finding price per unit*

Notes

1. Students need to be familiar with the formula $A = \ell \times w$.
2. Before the students start to work with their calculators, you may want them to estimate the answers.
3. Encourage students to compute mentally. The best method is to mentally determine the largest and smallest size for each price group, and then compute the cost for those rather than for all carpets in that range.

Extension

Have students find out the prices for different sizes of the same item at a local grocery store. Then have them compute the unit price for each size. Discuss why smaller sizes are usually more expensive and also why the "large economy size" is often *not* more economical.

1-50 Painting the Shed

Focus on . . .

- *Finding area*
- *Developing consumer skills*

Notes

1. Be sure students are able to compute the areas of rectangles and triangles.
2. This is a difficult problem. There are several sources of potential error: overhang on the roof, paint left in the can, some paint not suitable for exterior work, and so on. These factors could lead to a lively discussion.

1-51 MacDonald's Fence: Part I
1-52 MacDonald's Fence: Part II

Focus on . . .

- *Calculating area and ratio*

Notes

1. Students must have some familiarity with the formula $A = \ell \times w$ and understand perimeter before beginning this lesson.
2. Be sure students understand that the perimeter should be as small as possible. Discuss why this is so.

Extension

More able students may wish to examine the areas of triangular fields made from given lengths of fencing, and compare them with rectangular fields. They can then find which shape is more economical.

1-1

Keys to the Calculator's Heart

Learn what those buttons do

1. Take some time to investigate the various buttons on your calculator. Don't worry about buttons marked [M] [M+] [M−] [MC] [Ex] [↔]. Find out what the C and CE buttons do. (Hint: you might have to press the CE button twice.)

2. Try these problems:

a. 3 + 2 = _____ **b.** 9 − 4 = _____ **c.** 6 × 5 = _____ **d.** 35 ÷ 7 = _____

3. Now try these:

a. 14 + 22 + 3 **b.** 4752 − 637 **c.** 146 × 37 **d.** 32)2752

What you may have discovered:

Keys	Function
[1] [2] [3] [4] [5] [6] [7] [8] [9] [0]	Numeral Entry
[=]	Equals
[+]	Addition
[−]	Subtraction
[×]	Multiplication
[÷]	Division
[C/CE]	Clear All/Clear Entry
[%]	Percentage
[.]	Decimal Point

Calculation Examples

Function	Example	Key Entry Sequence	Display
Addition	123 + 45.6 =	[C] [C] [1] [2] [3] [+] [4] [5] [.] [6] =	168.6
Subtraction	123 − 45 =	[C] [C] [1] [2] [3] [−] [4] [5] =	78
Multiplication	12 × 34 =	[C] [C] [1] [2] [×] [3] [4] =	408
Division	125 ÷ 25 =	[C] [C] [1] [2] [5] [÷] [2] [5] =	5

Problem 3 Answers: **a.** 39 **b.** 4115 **c.** 5402 **d.** 86

• Introducing the calculator

Name ______________________________

1-2

The Speeding Addition Problem

Race against the clock

Find as many of the sums as you can in 3 min. The teacher will time you.
Use your calculator when necessary.

2 + 2 = ______	7 + 3 = ______	6 + 6 = ______
2 + 3 = ______	3 + 7 = ______	5 + 6 = ______
2 + 4 = ______	4 + 7 = ______	4 + 6 = ______
1 + 4 = ______	4 + 8 = ______	6 + 4 = ______
1 + 5 = ______	8 + 4 = ______	7 + 4 = ______
8 + 8 = ______	9 + 5 = ______	3 + 8 = ______
8 + 9 = ______	5 + 9 = ______	4 + 9 = ______
9 + 8 = ______	5 + 8 = ______	9 + 4 = ______
10 + 8 = ______	4 + 8 = ______	9 + 5 = ______
10 + 7 = ______	3 + 7 = ______	8 + 4 = ______
7 + 5 = ______	5 + 7 = ______	6 + 9 = ______
6 + 4 = ______	6 + 8 = ______	7 + 8 = ______
4 + 6 = ______	8 + 6 = ______	8 + 8 = ______
4 + 7 = ______	8 + 7 = ______	9 + 7 = ______
5 + 6 = ______	9 + 6 = ______	10 + 8 = ______
9 + 9 = ______	6 + 5 = ______	5 + 9 = ______
8 + 8 = ______	7 + 6 = ______	3 + 9 = ______
7 + 7 = ______	8 + 7 = ______	9 + 3 = ______
6 + 6 = ______	7 + 8 = ______	10 + 4 = ______
5 + 5 = ______	7 + 9 = ______	9 + 5 = ______

- ***Learning the calculator keys***
- ***Practicing addition facts***

Name ______________________

1-3

The Speeding Subtraction Problem

Review your subtraction facts

Try as many of these as you can in 3 min. The teacher will time you.
Use your calculator when you need it.

7 − 2 = ______	8 − 4 = ______	13 − 5 = ______
6 − 2 = ______	10 − 4 = ______	15 − 5 = ______
6 − 3 = ______	10 − 6 = ______	15 − 10 = ______
7 − 3 = ______	12 − 6 = ______	15 − 9 = ______
7 − 4 = ______	11 − 5 = ______	15 − 7 = ______
10 − 5 = ______	16 − 6 = ______	18 − 10 = ______
12 − 5 = ______	15 − 6 = ______	19 − 10 = ______
15 − 5 = ______	15 − 9 = ______	19 − 9 = ______
15 − 6 = ______	15 − 10 = ______	18 − 9 = ______
15 − 7 = ______	14 − 9 = ______	16 − 9 = ______
16 − 7 = ______	17 − 7 = ______	16 − 8 = ______
16 − 5 = ______	16 − 7 = ______	17 − 8 = ______
18 − 5 = ______	16 − 6 = ______	16 − 7 = ______
17 − 6 = ______	15 − 7 = ______	16 − 9 = ______
18 − 6 = ______	15 − 8 = ______	15 − 10 = ______
14 − 7 = ______	8 − 0 = ______	14 − 4 = ______
15 − 6 = ______	10 − 5 = ______	14 − 10 = ______
15 − 9 = ______	12 − 2 = ______	18 − 9 = ______
14 − 9 = ______	14 − 7 = ______	17 − 7 = ______
14 − 5 = ______	16 − 6 = ______	10 − 4 = ______

- ***Learning the calculator keys***
- ***Practicing subtraction facts***

Name ______________________________

1-4

The Speeding Multiplication Facts

A three-minute race

Find as many products as possible in 3 min., using your calculator when you cannot think of the answer.

0 × 3 = ______	2 × 9 = ______	7 × 4 = ______
3 × 4 = ______	3 × 9 = ______	4 × 7 = ______
4 × 3 = ______	4 × 9 = ______	5 × 7 = ______
9 × 3 = ______	9 × 4 = ______	6 × 7 = ______
9 × 2 = ______	8 × 4 = ______	6 × 6 = ______
5 × 6 = ______	4 × 8 = ______	10 × 9 = ______
6 × 5 = ______	3 × 8 = ______	9 × 9 = ______
6 × 4 = ______	8 × 3 = ______	9 × 8 = ______
7 × 4 = ______	7 × 3 = ______	8 × 9 = ______
8 × 4 = ______	7 × 2 = ______	7 × 9 = ______
9 × 7 = ______	5 × 5 = ______	7 × 8 = ______
8 × 7 = ______	6 × 5 = ______	8 × 8 = ______
7 × 8 = ______	6 × 6 = ______	8 × 7 = ______
6 × 8 = ______	7 × 6 = ______	8 × 6 = ______
5 × 8 = ______	7 × 7 = ______	5 × 6 = ______
3 × 2 = ______	5 × 6 = ______	5 × 8 = ______
7 × 6 = ______	5 × 8 = ______	3 × 6 = ______
6 × 7 = ______	8 × 8 = ______	6 × 3 = ______
7 × 7 = ______	9 × 9 = ______	8 × 6 = ______
1 × 5 = ______	8 × 2 = ______	6 × 8 = ______

- *Learning the calculator keys*
- *Practicing multiplication facts*

Name______________________________

1-5

The Speeding Division Facts

Another three-minute race

Do as many divisions as possible in 3 min.
Rely on your calculator when necessary.

9 ÷ 1 = ________
12 ÷ 3 = ________
12 ÷ 4 = ________
16 ÷ 4 = ________
20 ÷ 4 = ________

24 ÷ 8 = ________
24 ÷ 3 = ________
27 ÷ 3 = ________
30 ÷ 3 = ________
15 ÷ 3 = ________

80 ÷ 10 = ________
70 ÷ 10 = ________
70 ÷ 7 = ________
63 ÷ 7 = ________
56 ÷ 7 = ________

6 ÷ 6 = ________
12 ÷ 6 = ________
24 ÷ 6 = ________
48 ÷ 6 = ________
42 ÷ 6 = ________

20 ÷ 5 = ________
40 ÷ 5 = ________
50 ÷ 5 = ________
60 ÷ 10 = ________
70 ÷ 10 = ________

15 ÷ 5 = ________
30 ÷ 5 = ________
30 ÷ 6 = ________
36 ÷ 6 = ________
48 ÷ 6 = ________

56 ÷ 8 = ________
28 ÷ 4 = ________
16 ÷ 4 = ________
16 ÷ 2 = ________
8 ÷ 2 = ________

14 ÷ 7 = ________
28 ÷ 7 = ________
56 ÷ 7 = ________
49 ÷ 7 = ________
35 ÷ 7 = ________

70 ÷ 7 = ________
63 ÷ 7 = ________
63 ÷ 9 = ________
54 ÷ 9 = ________
27 ÷ 9 = ________

18 ÷ 9 = ________
18 ÷ 2 = ________
36 ÷ 4 = ________
72 ÷ 8 = ________
80 ÷ 8 = ________

10 ÷ 2 = ________
12 ÷ 2 = ________
24 ÷ 4 = ________
48 ÷ 8 = ________
48 ÷ 6 = ________

35 ÷ 5 = ________
40 ÷ 5 = ________
36 ÷ 6 = ________
64 ÷ 8 = ________
81 ÷ 9 = ________

- ***Learning the calculator keys***
- ***Practicing division facts***

Name ________________________________

1-6

The Great Mathematical Message

Accuracy will pay off

Now let's see if you can make the calculator calculate!
Try these exercises.

1. Use your answers to decode the messages.

a.

R	O	S	B	E	T	D	Y	U
1	2	3	4	5	6	7	8	9

$$\begin{array}{r} 8 \\ \times 9 \\ \hline \end{array} \qquad \begin{array}{r} 8569 \\ -\ 278 \\ \hline \end{array} \qquad \begin{array}{r} 252 \\ \times\ 18 \\ \hline \end{array}$$

____ _____ _____!

b.

E	I	C	R	T	H	M	N	K
1	2	3	4	5	6	7	8	9

$$\begin{array}{r} 1941 \\ \times\ \ 29 \\ \hline \end{array} \qquad \begin{array}{r} 614{,}238 \\ +101{,}185 \\ \hline \end{array}$$

_____ ______!

2. Complete the 4 operations.

To check your work, compute the sum of the 4 answers.
It should be a number with all digits the same.

a. 5843 + 4604 = __________ **b.** 794 × 42 = __________

c. 684 − 132 = __________ **d.** 1358 ÷ 14 = __________

- *Learning the calculator keys*
- *Practicing calculator operation*

*Name*________________________

1-7

Monster Math

Go carefully to get the picture

Join the answers, in the order given, to complete the picture.

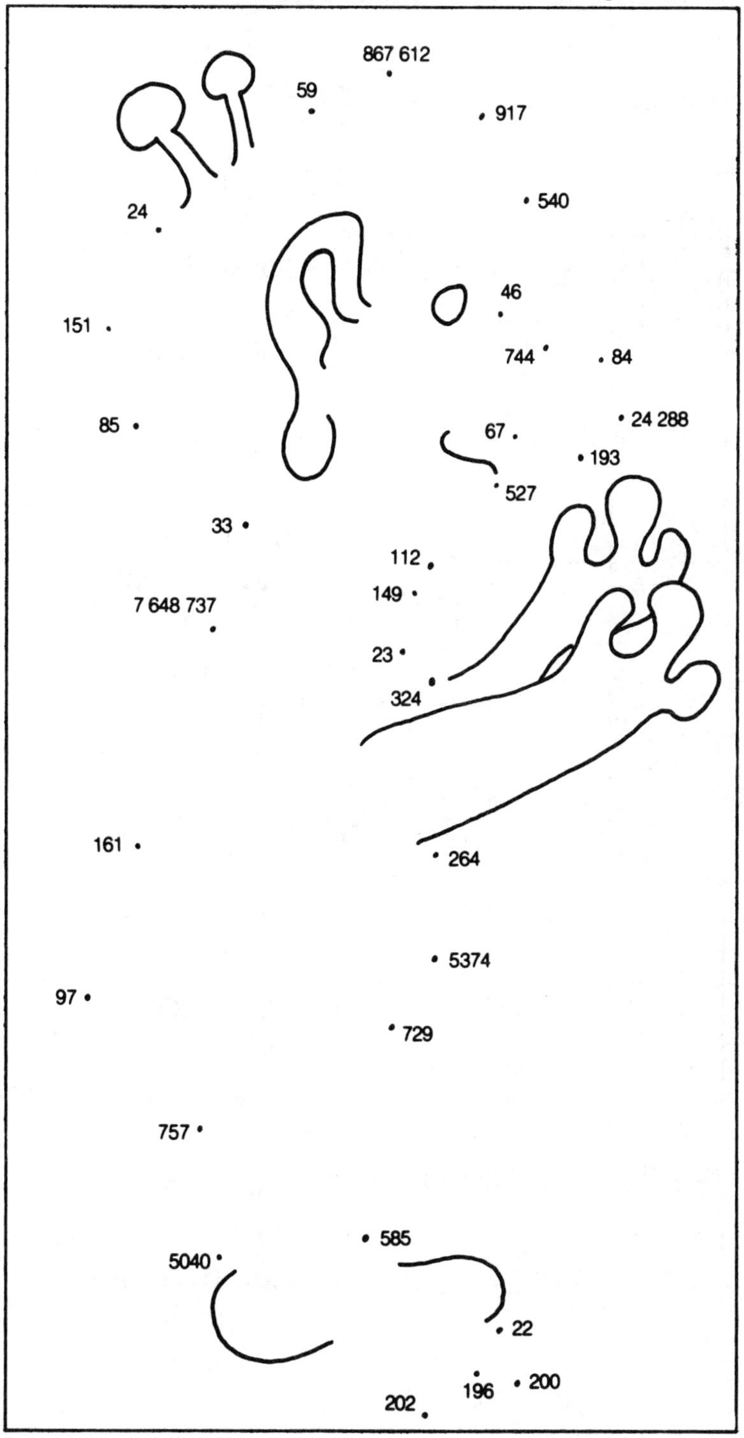

1. 6 × 54
2. 1288 ÷ 56
3. 84 + 65
4. 6 + 7 + 94 + 5
5. 654 − 127
6. 84 − 9 − 3 − 4 − 1
7. 97 + 64 + 32
8. 66 × 92 × 4
9. 5208 ÷ 62
10. 8 × 93
11. 6 × 7 + 4
12. 9 × 4 × 5 × 3
13. 965 − 48
14. 846,153 + 21,459
15. 708 ÷ 12
16. 8 + 7 + 6 + 3
17. 87 + 64
18. 3060 ÷ 36
19. 6 × 5 + 3
20. 7,651,498 − 2761
21. 7 × 23
22. 38 + 64 + 99 − 104
23. 1235 − 478
24. 6 × 7 × 4 × 5 × 3 × 2
25. 95 + 107
26. 14^2
27. 5200 ÷ 26
28. 5 × 4 + 2
29. 9 × 65
30. 9 × 9 × 9
31. 9617 − 4243
32. 66 + 66+ 66 +66

• Practicing calculator operation

Name ____________________

1-8

Crossnumber Puzzle

Will they all match up?

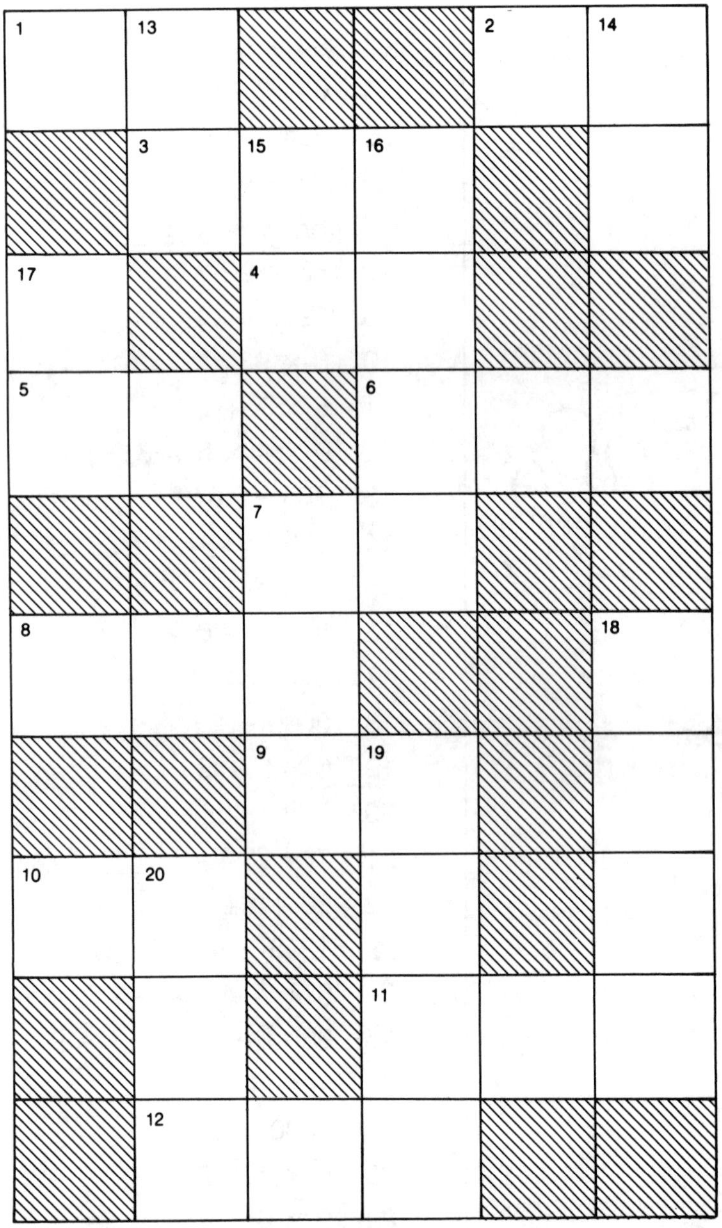

Across

1. 9 × 7
2. 37 + 25 + 20
3. 25 × 25 − 98
4. 9 × 6
5. 2881 ÷ 67
6. 87 × 3
7. 166 − 98
8. 76 × 4
9. 6 × 8 + 5
10. 44,415 ÷ 987
11. 25 × 17
12. 54 × 12

Down

7. 54 × 12 − 3
13. 7 × 5
14. 892 − 866
15. 5^2
16. 3561 + 2457 + 1410
17. 8^2
18. 1523 × 5
19. 7335 − 3587
20. 504,912 ÷ 942

• ***Developing speed and accuracy***

Name ______________________________

1-9

Calculator versus Calculator

Can you outthink the machine?

Time yourself!

1. Do the following problems *without* using the calculator.

Starting Time: _______

4 + 8 + 2 = _______	20 − 10 − 4 = _______	12 × 100 = _______
2 × 3 × 2 = _______	40 ÷ 5 ÷ 2 = _______	1500 ÷ 3 = _______

45	100	45	$4\overline{)120}$
+23	− 74	× 5	

Finishing Time: _______

Time needed *without* the calculator: _______

2. Do the following problems *using* the calculator instead of your head.

Starting Time: _______

3 + 6 + 5 = _______	25 − 5 − 7 = _______	16 × 100 = _______
4 × 3 × 4 = _______	30 ÷ 3 ÷ 5 = _______	1800 ÷ 3 = _______

52	100	62	$3\overline{)150}$
+34	− 67	× 6	

Finishing Time: _______

Time needed *using* the calculator: _______

• ***Using the calculator judiciously***

Name ____________________________________

1-10

The Great Turnover

Making numbers talk

To solve this crossword puzzle, do the arithmetic questions given as clues, and then invert the calculator. The numerals on the display will look like letters, and a word will be spelled. (Disregard the decimal point in the display.) Write these words in the correct spaces, as for a regular crossword puzzle.

Across

1. Three million, seven hundred eighty-one thousand, nine hundred thirty-seven
5. 191 × 11 × 18
8. $9^2 + 12$
9. 2542 + 1209
10. 1 ÷ 2
11. 17 × 3
12. 3 × 17 × 101
13. (400 − 3) × 9
16. 27,689 + 27,689
17. 0.3 × 3
19. 37 + 36
20. 5,380,000 − 81
23. 3 − 2.61
25. 5 × 15,469
27. 323 × 5 × 5 + 1000
29. 25 × 14 − 13
30. 1 − 0.63
33. 13 × 3
34. $2^3 \times 463 + 4010$
35. $300^3 + 10{,}819{,}173$
36. 7 × 11 × 2 × 2 × 2 × 5

Down

1. 2589 + 6894 + 21,475 + 4149
2. 80,000 − 22,281
3. 791 × 7
4. 1 − 0.07
5. 2 × 2 × 8777
6. 90,846 − 35,668
7. 30,000 + 1000 + 500 + 70 + 3
12. 23 × 23 + 242
14. 12 × 12 − 7
15. 331 + 331 + 331
16. 17 × 9 × 9 × 2 × 2 + 30
18. 1 − 0.630
20. 378,809 × 1
21. 9 × 3 × 167
22. 500 + 130 + 103
23. 3 × 1000 + 3 × 100 + 7 × 10 + 9 × 1
24. (10,000 + 9589) × 5 × 2 × 2
26. 9 + 0.37
28. 7 × 2 × 577 + 101
31. 35 × 23 − 32
32. $(5^2 + 12) \times 10$
34. 7 × 2

Beginning Calculator Math

- *Working with large numbers*
- *Developing speed and accuracy*

Name ____________________

1-11

Bigger Number Tips the Scales

Think bigger is "heavier"

Place each pair of numbers on the proper side of the balance.
The first example is done for you. Check with your calculator.

60 + 50	90 + 30
53 + 72	20 + 130
109 + 72	90 + 90
901 + 716	800 + 815
384 + 376	600 + 170
232 + 537	250 + 520
118 + 420	220 + 323
624 + 193	600 + 200
722 + 484	500 + 600
819 + 193	510 + 500
489 + 215	500 + 200
758 + 176	510 + 333

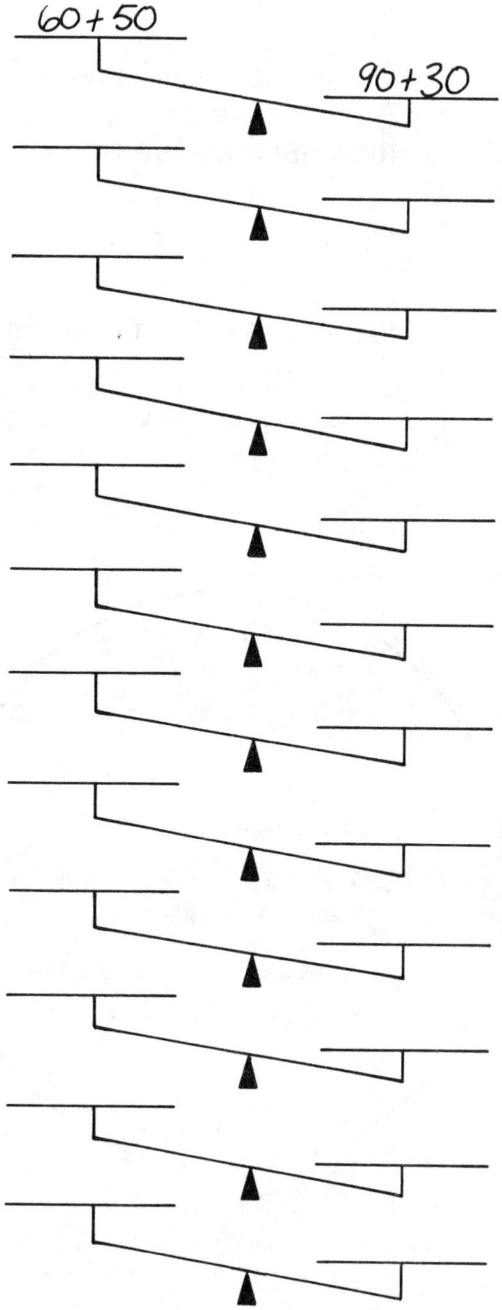

- ***Estimating in addition***
- ***Rounding to the nearest ten***
- ***Comparing sizes of numbers***

Name ______________________

1-12

Which is Greater?

The nearest hundred will get you close

Insert <, =, or > to make the statements true.
The first one is done for you.

161 + 253	<	272 + 249
353 + 496		420 + 510
109 + 672		391 + 314

910 + 716		815 + 627
384 + 376		616 + 123
232 + 537		255 + 351

118 + 420		323 + 622
624 + 193		262 + 345
722 + 484		560 + 444

819 + 193		515 + 497
489 + 215		521 + 812
758 + 176		333 + 614

Now check with your calculator.

- ***Estimating in addition***
- ***Rounding to the nearest ten or hundred***
- ***Comparing number values***

Name ____________________

One Lower

maller numbers

stimate the answer for each addition.
nallest sum in each triangle. Box the largest sum.
The first example is done for you.

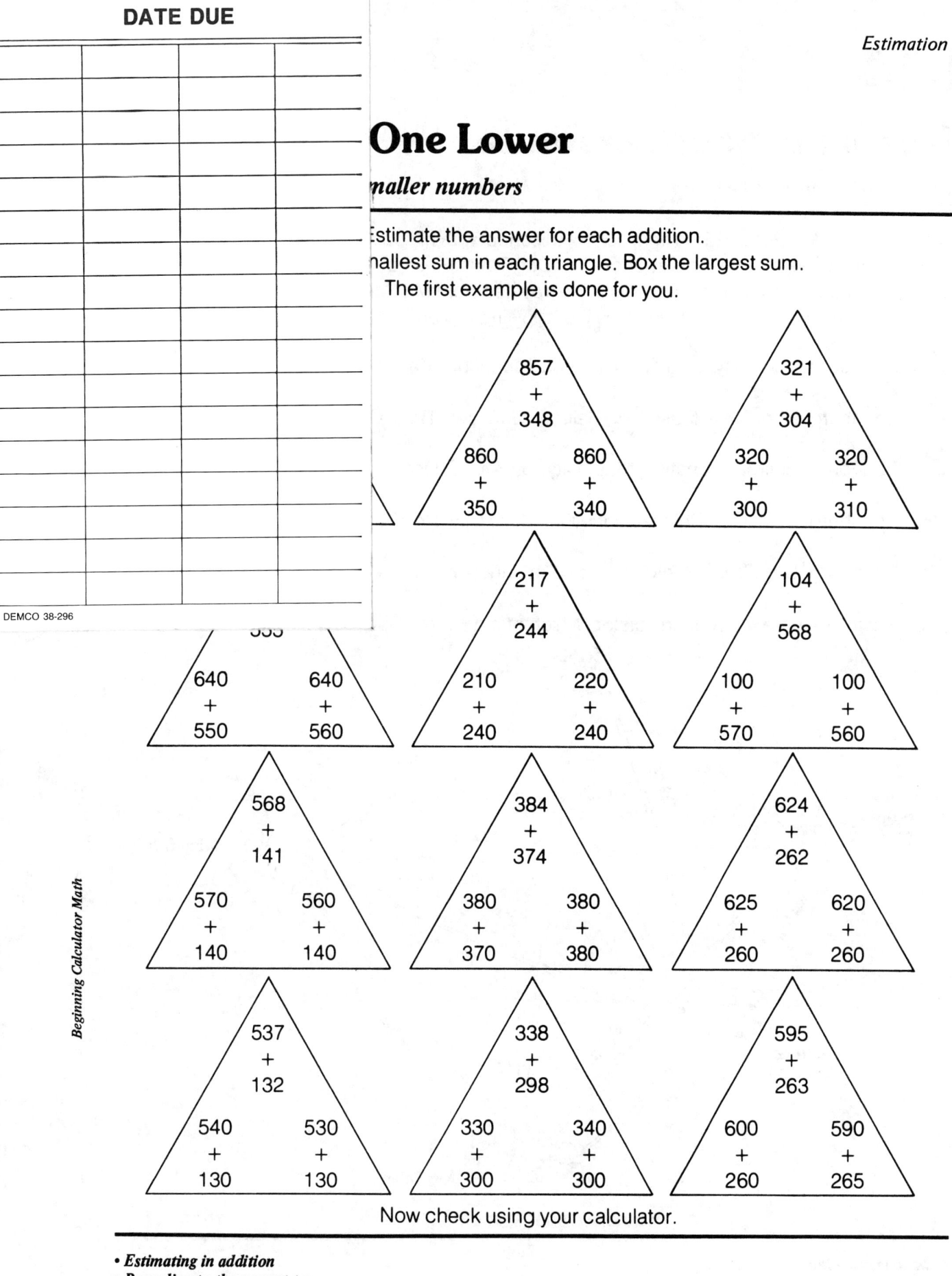

Problem	Estimate	Estimate
857 + 348	860 + 350	860 + 340
321 + 304	320 + 300	320 + 310
[illegible]	640 + 550	640 + 560
217 + 244	210 + 240	220 + 240
104 + 568	100 + 570	100 + 560
568 + 141	570 + 140	560 + 140
384 + 374	380 + 370	380 + 380
624 + 262	625 + 260	620 + 260
537 + 132	540 + 130	530 + 130
338 + 298	330 + 300	340 + 300
595 + 263	600 + 260	590 + 265

Now check using your calculator.

- ***Estimating in addition***
- ***Rounding to the nearest ten***

Name ______________________

1-14

Guess the Shortest Route

The nearest ten will help

Mr. Schulz goes from school to school with his puppet show. Next month, he will visit schools in Brick City, Dog Town, Railroad Junction, and Mass City. Using the map below, estimate the distance traveled from Mr. Schulz's home in Beanburg if he takes the following routes.

Estimates

1. Beanburg, Brick City, Dog Town, Railroad Junction, Mass City, Beanburg ________
2. Beanburg, Dog Town, Mass City, Railroad Junction, Brick City, Beanburg ________
3. Beanburg, Railroad Junction, Mass City, Brick City, Dog Town, Beanburg ________
4. Beanburg, Brick City, Railroad Junction, Mass City, Dog Town, Beanburg ________
5. Beanburg, Dog Town, Brick City, Railroad Junction, Mass City, Beanburg ________

Check the results with your calculator. Which of the 5 routes is the shortest? ________ .

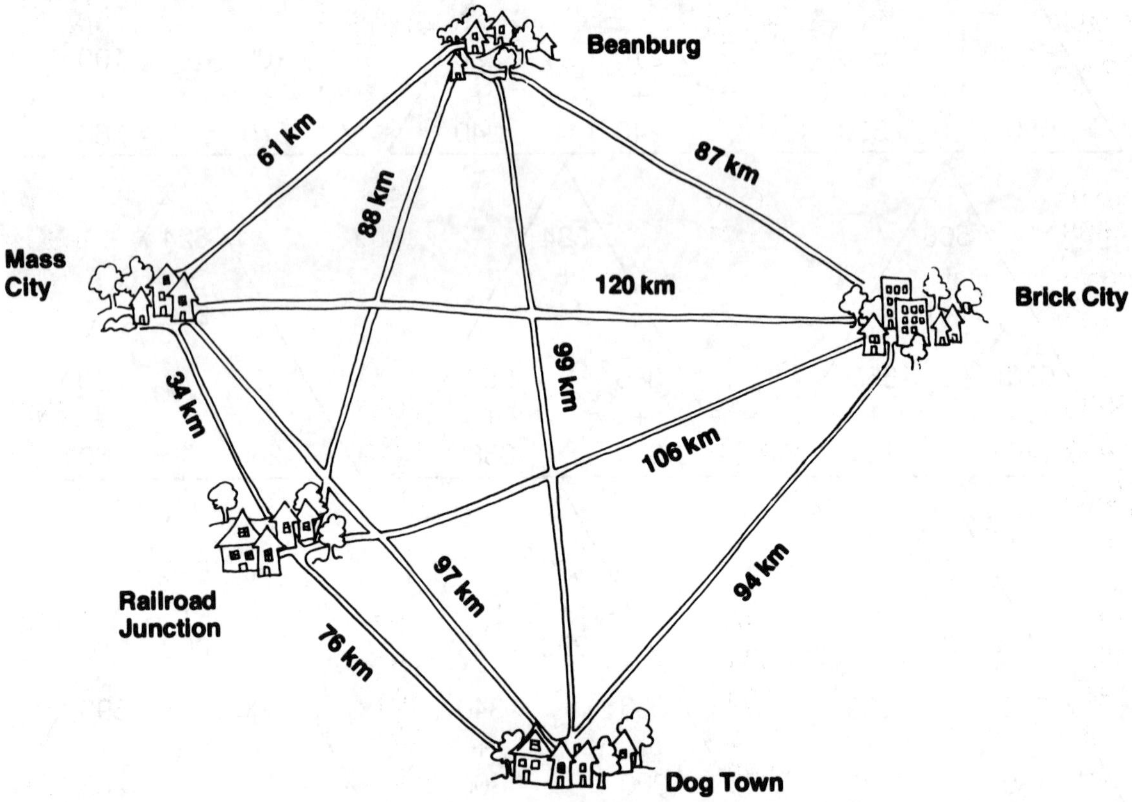

Is there a shorter route?

- ***Estimating in addition***
- ***Rounding***
- ***Reading maps***

Name ________________________________

Beginning Calculator Math

1-15

How Many Hundreds: Part I

Estimate, then calculate

Estimate to the nearest hundred. When you finish the page, calculate the exact answers to see how close you were.

320 +429 700	204 +127	389 +413	790 +538
449 +683 1100	255 +840	145 +579	421 +296
2681 +582 3300	1525 +766	868 +1304	4939 +873
2810 +4688 7500	1599 +1001	2945 +5496	1615 +9584
8535 +865 9400	542 +5715	3087 +756	9499 +192
323 355 184 9 + 34 900	10 474 54 8 +595	33 91 101 192 + 64	109 77 63 50 + 71

- ***Estimating in addition***
- ***Rounding to the nearest hundred***
- ***Adding four-digit numbers***

Name ______________________________

1-16

How Many Hundreds: Part II

Rounding makes it faster

Estimate to the nearest hundred. When you finish the page, calculate the exact answers to see how close you were.

546 + 471 = About 1000

372 + 106 = ______________

211 + 934 = ______________

120 + 586 = ______________

111 + 373 = ______________

7898 + 7355 = About 15,000

4494 + 2214 = ______________

2557 + 1215 = ______________

1454 + 9506 = ______________

8278 + 3760 = ______________

71 + 886 = About 1000

409 + 696 = ______________

232 + 38 = ______________

32 + 645 = ______________

753 + 650 = ______________

4710 + 229 = About 4900

867 + 6263 = ______________

4936 + 6193 = ______________

280 + 8837 = ______________

1598 + 817 = ______________

15 + 98 + 7 + 90 + 32 + 7 + 5 + 2 + 27 = About 300

517 + 38 + 9 + 5 + 953 + 3 + 29 + 7 = ______________

54 + 22 + 565 + 7 + 5 + 3 + 85 + 33 = ______________

17 + 554 + 491 + 998 + 83 + 4 + 11 = ______________

568 + 319 + 30 + 32 + 3362 + 24 + 104 = ______________

- ***Estimating in addition***
- ***Rounding to the nearest hundred***
- ***Adding four-digit numbers***

Name ______________________________

1-17

About the Same

Think rounding to tens

Join a subtraction phrase from the left-hand column to one that will have approximately the same answer in the right-hand column.
Circle the one you think has the larger answer.
An example has been done for you.

87 – 23	270 – 30
255 – 63	250 – 60
145 – 57	540 – 170
270 – 28	620 – 480
152 – 106	520 – 210
759 – 379	150 – 110
517 – 213	410 – 220
539 – 167	90 – 20
447 – 252	150 – 60
408 – 218	880 – 340
877 – 344	760 – 380
623 – 484	450 – 250

Check with your calculator.

- ***Estimating in subtraction***
- ***Rounding to the nearest ten***
- ***Subtracting three-digit numbers***

Name ____________________

1-18

Speedy Subtraction: Part I

Think in tens and hundreds

Estimation

Write down your estimates.

```
  653     Think        104    Think       595          338
-  47     650         - 68    100        - 63         - 90
          -50                 -70
          600
```

```
  819             716             624            355
 -192            -109            -262           -193
```

```
 6542            6484            2118           1205
 -671           -3722           -1120           -163
```

```
 6857            5716            9915           9094
-1348           -3901           - 221          -4089
```

```
  890            6112             132         75,321
-  40           -2326            - 37         -   304
```

```
  563          24,384             916           2555
 -428          -   374           - 44           -637
```

Now check your estimates using the calculator.

- **Estimating in subtraction**
- **Rounding to the nearest ten or hundred**

28   Name

1-19

Speedy Subtraction: Part II

Look for the tens

Write down your estimates.

255 − 63 = About 200

145 − 41 = ______

827 − 57 = ______

470 − 49 = ______

267 − 26 = ______

294 − 213 = About 80

401 − 167 = ______

539 − 308 = ______

447 − 175 = ______

998 − 259 = ______

152 − 99 = About 50

280 − 106 = ______

759 − 243 = ______

908 − 879 = ______

886 − 517 = ______

798 − 56 = About 740

323 − 17 = ______

879 − 183 = ______

104 − 62 = ______

8707 − 33 = ______

338 − 19 − 71 − 76 − 8 − 109 = About 60

623 − 90 − 53 − 35 − 198 − 4 = ______

201 − 98 − 36 − 11 − 49 − 7 = ______

822 − 2 − 168 − 81 − 1 − 204 = ______

685 − 31 − 53 − 7 − 3 − 99 = ______

Now check your estimates using the calculator.

- ***Estimating in subtraction***
- ***Rounding to the nearest ten or hundred***

Name ______

1-20

Find the Smaller Number

Watch for those small differences

Put an X next to the subtraction sentence (A or B) which will give the smallest answer.
Put an X in both columns if the two answers are the same.
Do not work out the differences. Instead, carefully compare the sentences.
You may check your guesses with the calculator.

A	X	B	X
685 – 299		680 – 299	
502 – 159		502 – 160	
847 – 274		850 – 274	
668 – 320		670 – 322	
320 – 232		320 – 230	
447 – 111		450 – 111	
784 – 310		780 – 310	
550 – 300		550 – 295	
680 – 300		685 – 300	
847 – 270		850 – 270	
950 – 480		951 – 477	
822 – 510		822 – 513	

A	X	B	X
670 – 320		668 – 322	
447 – 110		450 – 110	
846 – 470		850 – 468	
554 – 300		554 – 295	
480 – 240		479 – 244	
324 – 232		324 – 230	
950 – 477		951 – 480	
780 – 308		784 – 308	
850 – 470		846 – 468	
820 – 510		820 – 513	
479 – 240		480 – 244	
500 – 159		500 – 160	

- ***Estimating in subtraction***
- ***Comparing subtraction sentences***
- ***Adjusting for rounding error***

Name ______________________________

1-21

Round and Multiply

Think with tens again

Circle the best estimate. Check with your calculator.

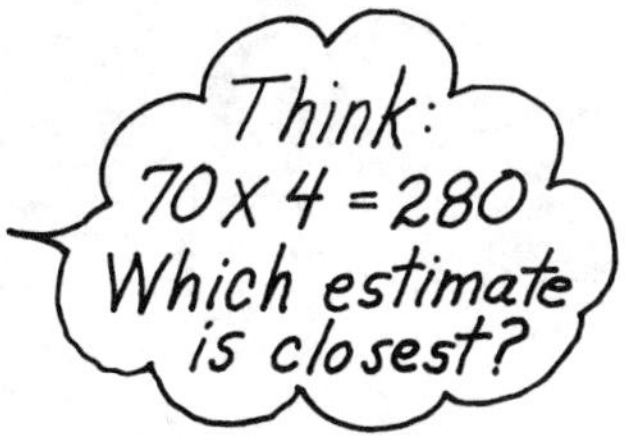
Think:
70 X 4 = 280
Which estimate is closest?

Product	Estimates		
73 × 4	250	300	350
92 × 5	400	450	500
81 × 7	600	700	800
29 × 5	150	200	250
54 × 6	200	250	300
66 × 4	250	300	350
79 × 8	600	650	700
49 × 7	350	400	450
95 × 6	500	550	600
38 × 9	350	375	400
56 × 3	150	175	200
67 × 8	450	500	550

- ***Estimating in multiplication***
- ***Rounding to the nearest ten***
- ***Multiplying rounded numbers***

Name ____________________

1-22

Easy Multiplication

Think rounding first

Record your estimate first, then calculate.

62 × 3 186 Think: 60 × 3 (180)	35 × 4 Think: 40 × 4 (160)	18 × 6 ______ ( )	93 × 7 ______ ( )
104 × 6 ______ ( )	594 × 7 ______ ( )	338 × 5 ______ ( )	623 × 8 ______ ( )
32 × 29 ______ ( )	18 × 37 ______ ( )	42 × 35 ______ ( )	84 × 63 ______ ( )
429 × 35 ______ ( )	114 × 85 ______ ( )	653 × 57 ______ ( )	371 × 93 ______ ( )
684 × 91 ______ ( )	389 × 70 ______ ( )	221 × 73 ______ ( )	126 × 16 ______ ( )

Now check your estimates on the calculator.

- ***Estimating in multiplication***
- ***Rounding to the nearest ten or hundred***

Name ______________________________

1-23

Guess One Higher, One Lower

Choose your challenge well

Write down your estimate for the range into which the product will fall.
Make the range as small as you dare.
Check by finding the exact product (P) with your calculator.

Step 1

Step 2

	P > ?	Exact Product (P)	P < ?
94 × 6	540	564	600
53 × 7			
61 × 8			
89 × 5			
83 × 9			
74 × 3			
49 × 4			
83 × 5			
7 × 49			
6 × 37			
8 × 21			
6 × 94			
7 × 83			
5 × 42			
9 × 63			
4 × 91			

- ***Estimating in multiplication***
- ***Rounding to the nearest ten***

Name ______________________

1-24

Code Puzzle

Find the closest estimate

Guess the product and place the corresponding letter in the appropriate box.
The first one is done for you.
You may use your calculator to check your guess.

1.

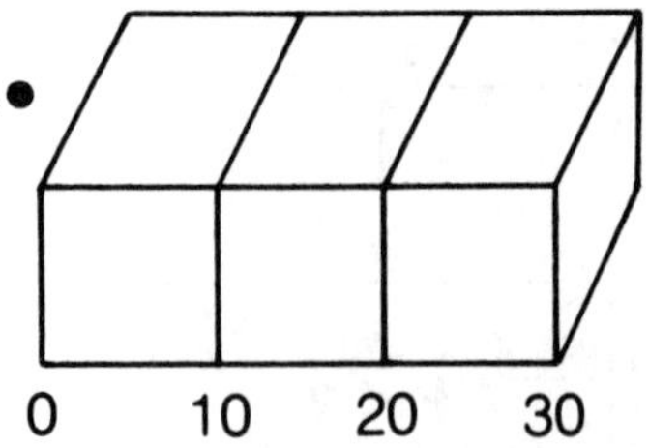

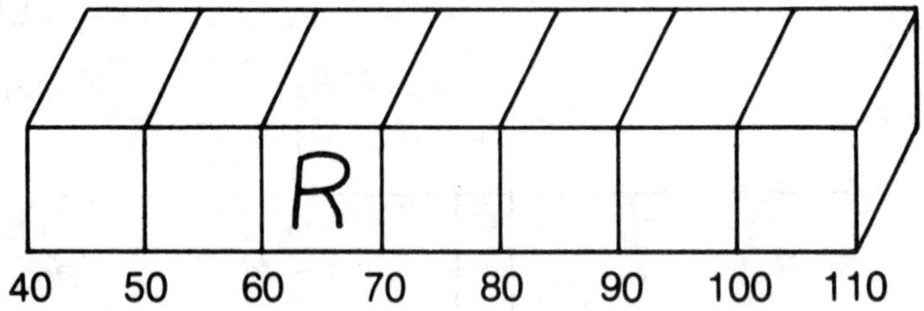

R 9 × 7
R 9 × 8
O 2 × 3
O 13 × 4
T 21 × 5

E 6 × 4
E 12 × 7
C 12 × 4
C 14 × 7
N 9 × 2

2.

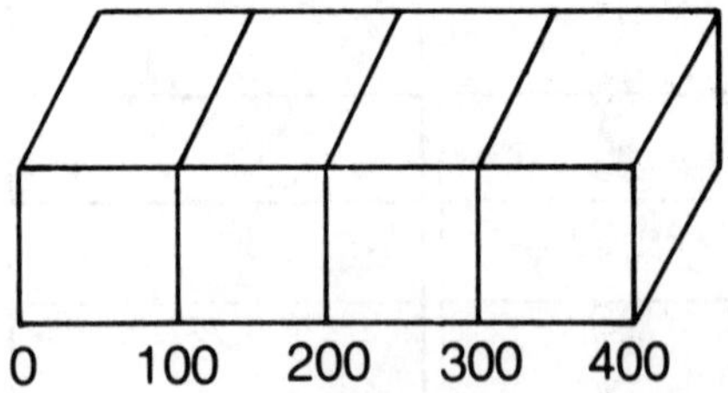

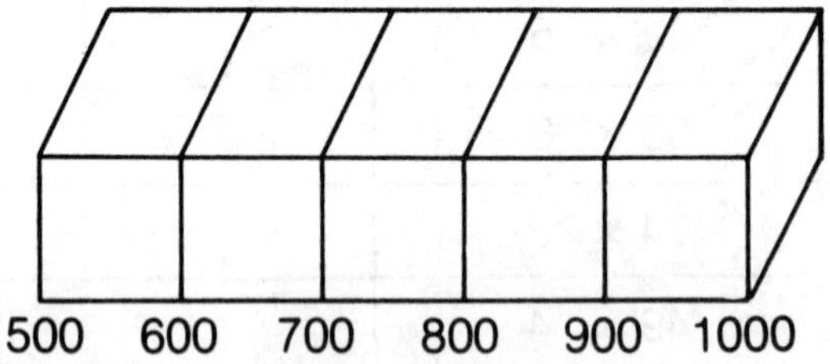

E 42 × 6
E 46 × 3
K 27 × 3
N 95 × 9
P 67 × 5

O 77 × 8
I 83 × 9
G 89 × 6
G 34 × 29

3.

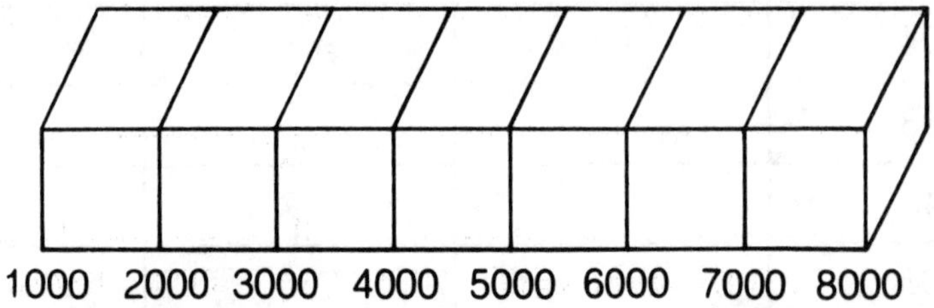

E 61 × 42
E 89 × 62
T 76 × 95
F 58 × 77

R 421 × 9
P 365 × 4
C 942 × 7

- *Estimating in multiplication*
- *Rounding to the nearest ten or hundred*

Name ______________________________

Beginning Calculator Math

1-25

Number Line Puzzle

Find the message on the line

Estimate the products. Put the corresponding letter in the correct place on the number line. The first example is done for you. If arranged correctly, the letters will spell a sentence. (Be careful! Sometimes you will have 2 letters in the same range.)

Letter	Product
O	91 × 60
K	58 × 70
S	59 × 80
I	89 × 50
T	83 × 90
L	74 × 30
A	49 × 40
E	81 × 81
R	79 × 78
R	60 × 95
L	70 × 37
R	40 × 96
O	50 × 74
C	90 × 57
C	90 × 75
W	52 × 62

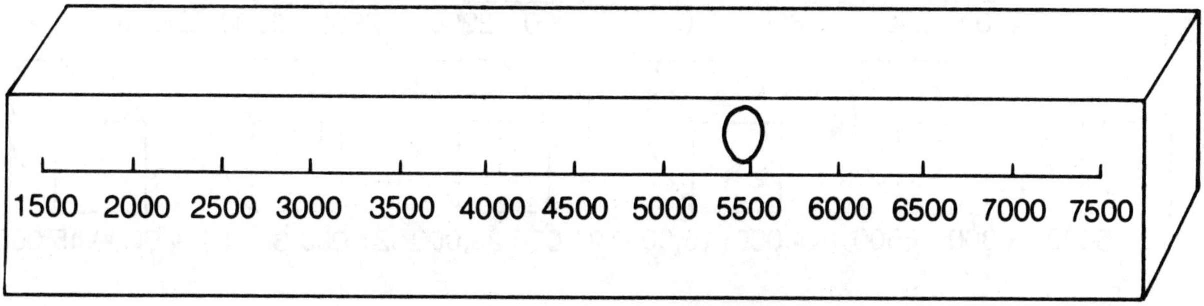

If necessary, check your estimates with your calculator.

- ***Estimating in multiplication***
- ***Adjusting for rounding error***
- ***Using a number line***

Name ________________________________

1-26

The Hidden Message

Find out what you are

Estimate the range into which the products will fall.
Place the corresponding letter on the cube labeled with that range.
If marked correctly, the cubes will spell out a sentence.

67 × 40	**E**	47 × 3	**Y**
37 × 60	**V**	40 × 71	**R**
300 × 74	**V**	300 × 96	**E**
80 × 23	**E**	70 × 42	**Y**
94 × 7	**U**	56 × 7	**O**
41 × 40	**R**	37 × 40	**A**
92 × 60	**C**	92 × 70	**L**
900 × 46	**R**	400 × 36	**E**

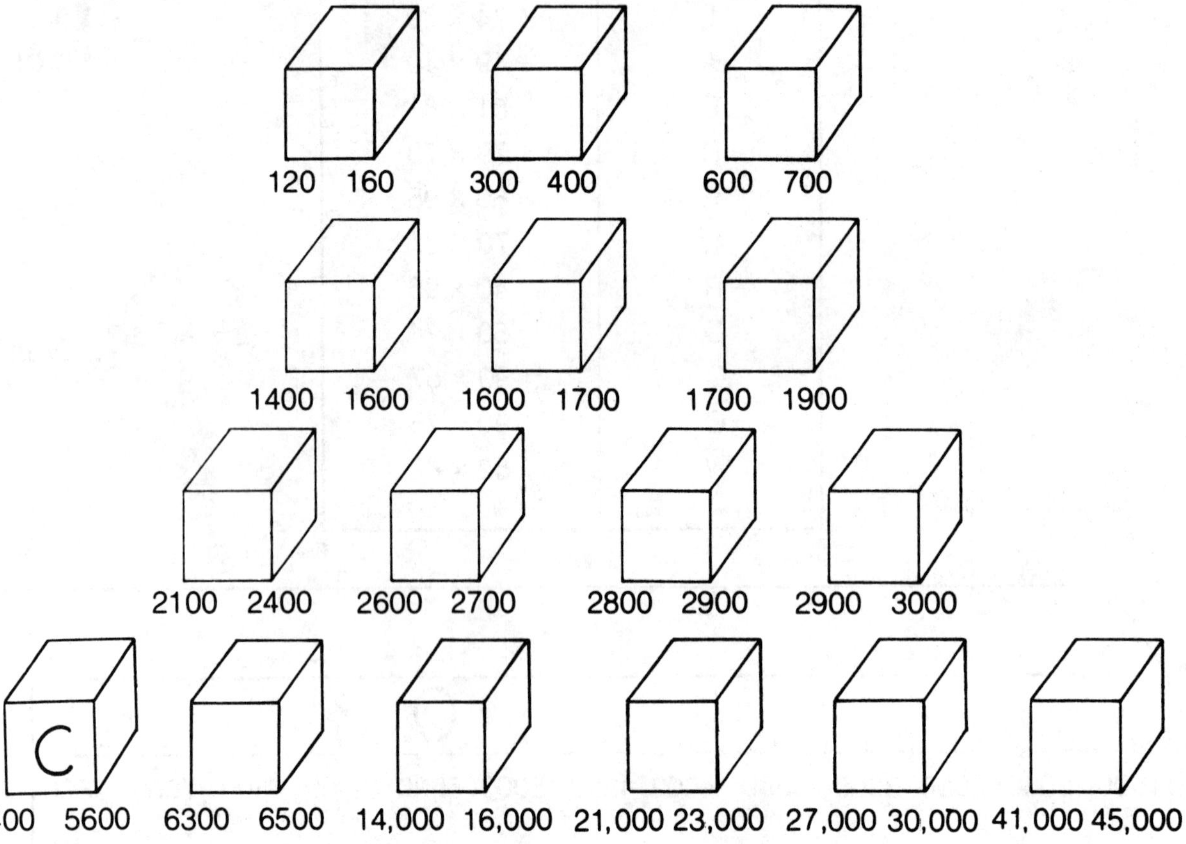

If necessary, check your estimates with your calculator.

• Estimating in multiplication

Name ______________________________

1-27

Whiz Quiz

How fast, how close?

Write your estimates.

Think
80×6=480

1.
81 × 6 = ______
53 × 9 = ______
31 × 7 = ______
48 × 5 = ______
87 × 8 = ______

2.
20 × 51 = ______
28 × 88 = ______
41 × 96 = ______
97 × 46 = ______
65 × 23 = ______

3.
333 × 597 = ______
420 × 874 = ______
530 × 983 = ______
845 × 160 = ______
106 × 627 = ______

4.
508 × 7 = ______
641 × 8 = ______
809 × 6 = ______
128 × 9 = ______
626 × 5 = ______

5.
827 × 27 = ______
131 × 76 = ______
166 × 61 = ______
209 × 58 = ______
644 × 26 = ______

6.
1346 × 8 = ______
2015 × 8 = ______
1946 × 3 = ______
4901 × 90 = ______
2855 × 70 = ______

Now check your estimates with the calculator.

- ***Estimating in multiplication***
- ***Rounding to the nearest ten or hundred***

Name ______

1-28

Quick Parts

What's about half or a third?

Find approximately 1/2 of the given values.
An example is done for you.

823 ⟶ 400

616 ⟶ ______

187 ⟶ ______

1375 ⟶ ______

779 ⟶ ______

Find approximately 1/3 of the given values.
An example is done for you.

311 ⟶ 100

589 ⟶ ______

277 ⟶ ______

688 ⟶ ______

897 ⟶ ______

Find approximately 1/4 of the following numbers.
An example is done for you.

523 ⟶ 125

920 ⟶ ______

643 ⟶ ______

162 ⟶ ______

369 ⟶ ______

1/3 of 313 is approximately: ______

1/4 of 554 is approximately: ______

1/2 of 233 is approximately: ______

1/4 of 981 is approximately: ______

1/2 of 506 is approximately: ______

1/3 of 624 is approximately: ______

2/3 of 173 is approximately: ______

1/2 of 726 is approximately: ______

1/4 of 266 is approximately: ______

3/4 of 307 is approximately: ______

1/3 of 496 is approximately: ______

1/2 of 544 is approximately: ______

2/3 of 267 is approximately: ______

3/4 of 806 is approximately: ______

1/4 of 963 is approximately: ______

1/3 of 354 is approximately: ______

• *Estimating fractional parts*

Name ______

1-29

The Educated Guess: Part I

Decide if it's really more or less

Write your estimate and indicate by + or − whether you expect the quotient to be greater than (+) or less than (−) the estimate. Then use your calculator to determine the quotient, and record it (to the nearest whole number) in the chart. Time: 6 min.

	Estimate	Quotient
695 ÷ 7	100-	99
323 ÷ 6	50+	54
388 ÷ 3		
124 ÷ 2		
151 ÷ 4		
889 ÷ 9		
554 ÷ 9		
838 ÷ 2		
522 ÷ 3		
326 ÷ 7		
191 ÷ 4		
119 ÷ 9		
745 ÷ 8		
465 ÷ 4		
703 ÷ 7		
413 ÷ 7		
257 ÷ 6		
160 ÷ 3		
100 ÷ 8		
625 ÷ 6		

	Estimate	Quotient
943 ÷ 2		
158 ÷ 9		
366 ÷ 5		
228 ÷ 5		
142 ÷ 4		
203 ÷ 3		
126 ÷ 8		
790 ÷ 6		
493 ÷ 4		
307 ÷ 8		
438 ÷ 4		
273 ÷ 6		
170 ÷ 4		
106 ÷ 8		
663 ÷ 5		
390 ÷ 3		
589 ÷ 4		
367 ÷ 4		
229 ÷ 6		
143 ÷ 3		

• ***Estimating in division***

Name ____________________

1-30

The Educated Guess: Part II

Judge the error in your estimates

Write your estimate and indicate whether
you expect the exact answer to be greater than or less than the estimate.

	Estimate	Quotient		Estimate	Quotient
606 ÷ 2	300+	303	65.3 ÷ 5		
34.4 ÷ 4			370 ÷ 3		
195 ÷ 5			21 ÷ 5		
11 ÷ 5			119 ÷ 4		
62.9 ÷ 7			677 ÷ 9		
3.84 ÷ 6			414 ÷ 5		
21.8 ÷ 8			23.5 ÷ 3		
123 ÷ 3			13.3 ÷ 4		
70.3 ÷ 7			75.7 ÷ 6		
399 ÷ 2			430 ÷ 6		
244 ÷ 5			26.2 ÷ 9		
13.8 ÷ 6			14.9 ÷ 2		
7.86 ÷ 5			84.7 ÷ 3		
44.6 ÷ 3			12.7 ÷ 8		
253 ÷ 7			154 ÷ 9		
2.95 ÷ 7			278 ÷ 6		
787 ÷ 4			74.1 ÷ 2		
20.9 ÷ 8			197 ÷ 4		
39.4 ÷ 7			5.24 ÷ 3		
104 ÷ 4			13.9 ÷ 9		

• Estimating in division

Name ____________________

1-31

The Line-Up

Visualize your answer on the line

Write the letter for each division problem in its proper place on the number line. The first one is done for you.

1.

a.	435 ÷ 6	**e.**	429 ÷ 12
b.	74.1 ÷ 9	**f.**	760 ÷ 7
c.	627 ÷ 7	**g.**	325 ÷ 15
d.	123 ÷ 2	**h.**	81.5 ÷ 5

a

0 10 20 30 40 50 60 70 80 90 100 110 120

2.

a.	274 ÷ 13	**e.**	346 ÷ 6
b.	791 ÷ 8	**f.**	262 ÷ 3
c.	23.5 ÷ 17	**g.**	190 ÷ 1.8
d.	961 ÷ 30	**h.**	275 ÷ 4

0 10 20 30 40 50 60 70 80 90 100 110 120

3.

a.	210 ÷ 6	**e.**	46.2 ÷ 79
b.	967 ÷ 9	**f.**	266 ÷ 12
c.	443 ÷ 8	**g.**	896 ÷ 20
d.	128 ÷ 8.1	**h.**	598 ÷ 6.7

0 10 20 30 40 50 60 70 80 90 100 110 120

- *Estimating in division*
- *Rounding to the nearest whole number*

Name ______________________

1-32

Checking the Facts

A game of speed and accuracy (for 1 player)

Equipment

Set of mini-cards at the right
(Cut them up
and put them in a little box.)
Calculator
Score sheet (below)
Pencil

Instructions

1. Take out one card, and enter the addition on it (say, 4 + 5) into the calculator.
   Don't push the [=] button!
2. Say the answer to yourself.
3. Push the [=] button and check.
4. Record your score (right or wrong) on the score sheet.
5. Continue, until all the mini-cards are used up.

Right	Wrong

8 + 6	3 + 2	9 + 2	6 + 8
4 + 9	7 + 9	1 + 3	4 + 4
1 + 8	0 + 4	4 + 5	3 + 9
4 + 3	3 + 8	7 + 4	0 + 8
2 + 0	9 + 4	0 + 6	1 + 0
9 + 7	4 + 6	9 + 5	9 + 8
5 + 2	1 + 7	4 + 7	1 + 9
6 + 2	4 + 8	0 + 5	7 + 7
1 + 5	0 + 2	5 + 9	8 + 4
7 + 8	4 + 2	7 + 6	2 + 9
2 + 4	0 + 3	8 + 2	3 + 6
6 + 3	5 + 6	0 + 9	5 + 0
3 + 3	7 + 3	7 + 1	9 + 9
9 + 6	1 + 1	2 + 6	6 + 7
2 + 8	9 + 0	8 + 7	2 + 2
5 + 3	3 + 4	4 + 1	8 + 3
4 + 0	8 + 1	6 + 5	1 + 2
6 + 1	0 + 0	2 + 3	6 + 9
5 + 7	5 + 8	1 + 6	7 + 5
5 + 5	6 + 6	7 + 2	1 + 4
9 + 3	9 + 1	3 + 0	8 + 5
5 + 4	6 + 0	8 + 9	2 + 7
8 + 8	8 + 0	2 + 1	0 + 1
7 + 0	3 + 5	5 + 2	3 + 7
3 + 1	0 + 7	6 + 4	5 + 1

• *Reviewing addition facts*

Name ________________________________

1-33

The Nimble-Minded Adder

Learn to play Addnim (for 2 players)

Equipment

Calculator Score sheets (below) Pencil

Instructions

1. Pick a "target" number between 25 and 50 (for example, 38).
2. Player A punches in a one-digit number (1, 2, 3, 4, 5, 6, 7, 8, or 9).
3. Player B adds a single digit number to A's number.
4. Players take turns adding one-digit numbers until one player hits the target.
5. The student who reaches the target (38) wins the round.
6. Play several rounds. Keep a record on your score sheet.

Example: Target: 38

Player	Action	Display	
A	7	7	
B	+ 6	13	
A	+ 9	22	
B	+ 8	30	
A	+ 8	38	← The Winner

P.S.: There is a "strategy" for this game. If you find it, you can win every time!

P.P.S.: Your teacher has the rules for "variations" of this game. Ask.

Round	Player A: ________	Player B: ________
1		
2		
3		
4		
5		
6		
7		
8		
9		
10		

Round	Player A: ________	Player B: ________
1		
2		
3		
4		
5		
6		
7		
8		
9		
10		

- ***Reviewing addition facts***
- ***Detecting patterns***
- ***Developing strategies***

Name ________________________________

1-34

The Nimble-Minded Subtractor

Learn to play Subnim (for 2 players)

Equipment

Calculator Score sheets (below) Pencil

Instructions

1. Pick a "starter" number between 25 and 50 (say, 38). Enter it into your calculator.
2. Player A subtracts a one-digit number (1, 2, 3, 4, 5, 6, 7, 8, or 9) from the starter.
3. Player B then subtracts a one-digit number from the new remainder.
4. Players take turns subtracting one-digit numbers until one player hits 0.
5. The player who reaches 0 wins the round.
6. Play several rounds. Keep a record on your score sheet.

Example: Starter: 38

Player	Action	Display
		38
A	− 6	32
B	− 9	23
A	− 8	15
B	− 1	14
A	− 5	9
B	− 9	0 ← The Winner

P.S.: There is a "strategy" for this game. If you find it, you can win every time.

P.P.S.: Your teacher has the rules for "variations" of this game. Ask.

Round	Player A: ________	Player B: ________
1		
2		
3		
4		
5		
6		
7		
8		
9		
10		

Round	Player A: ________	Player B: ________
1		
2		
3		
4		
5		
6		
7		
8		
9		
10		

- ***Reviewing subtraction facts***
- ***Reviewing multiplication facts***
- ***Detecting patterns***
- ***Developing strategies***

Name ____________________

1-35

The Nimble-Minded Multiplier

Learn to play Multnim (for 2 players)

Equipment

Calculator Score Sheets (below) Pencil

Instructions

1. Pick a "target" number around 1000 (for example, 960).
2. Player A enters a one-digit number into the calculator.
3. Player B then multiplies this by another one-digit number. Multiplying by 1 is not allowed.
4. Players take turns multiplying by one-digit numbers until one player reaches (or passes) the target.
5. The player who reaches the target **loses** the round.
6. Play several rounds. Keep a record on your score sheet.

Example Target: 960

Player	Action	Display	
A	[2]	2	
B	[×] [4]	8	
A	[×] [7]	56	
B	[×] [2]	112	
A	[×] [5]	560	
B	[×] [2]	1120	← The Loser

P.S.: There is a "strategy" for this game. If you find it, you can win every time!

P.P.S.: Your teacher has the rules for variations of this game. Ask.

Round	Player A: ______	Player B: ______
1		
2		
3		
4		
5		
6		
7		
8		
9		
10		

Round	Player A: ______	Player B: ______
1		
2		
3		
4		
5		
6		
7		
8		
9		
10		

- ***Reviewing multiplication facts***
- ***Reviewing division facts***
- ***Detecting patterns***
- ***Developing strategies***

Name ______________________________

1-36

The Nimble-Minded Divider

Learn to play Divnim (for 2 players)

Equipment

Calculator Score sheets (below) Pencil

Instructions

1. Pick as a "starter" number a multiple of 100 between 1000 and 10,000 (say, 1200). Enter the number into your calculator.
2. Player A divides the starter by a one-digit number.
3. Player B then divides the new answer by another one-digit number. Division by 1 is not allowed.
4. Play continues until one player's answer contains a decimal. (It didn't divide evenly.)
5. The player with a decimal in the answer **loses** the round.
6. Play several rounds. Keep a record on your score sheet.

Example Starter: 1200

Player	Action	Display	
		1200	
A	÷ 4	300	
B	÷ 5	60	
A	÷ 8	7.5	← The Loser

P.S.: There is a "strategy" for this game. If you find it, you can win every time.

P.P.S.: Your teacher has the rules for "variations" of this game. Ask.

Round	Player A:	Player B:
1		
2		
3		
4		
5		
6		
7		
8		
9		
10		

Round	Player A:	Player B:
1		
2		
3		
4		
5		
6		
7		
8		
9		
10		

- *Developing factoring skills*
- *Reviewing division facts*
- *Detecting patterns*
- *Developing strategies*

Name ______________________________

1-37

Mental Magic

It's all in your mind

(for 1 to 4 players)

Equipment

1 score sheet per player (below)
Calculator
Pencils
Flap over the calculator display

Instructions

1. Punch in a string of 4 numbers and 3 operations, (say (3 + 2 − 4) × 7) while your partners watch.
2. All players write down their answers on their own score sheets.
3. Press [=], lift the flap and check your answers.
4. Take turns punching in questions, until the score sheets are filled.
5. The player with the most correct answers is the winner.

(Tape over display)
FLAP

ANSWER BELOW
Don't look until all answers are written!

Name:	
Round	**Answer**
1	
2	
3	
4	
5	
6	
7	
8	
9	
10	
11	
12	
Number Correct:	

Name:	
Round	**Answer**
1	
2	
3	
4	
5	
6	
7	
8	
9	
10	
11	
12	
Number Correct:	

Name:	
Round	**Answer**
1	
2	
3	
4	
5	
6	
7	
8	
9	
10	
11	
12	
Number Correct:	

Name:	
Round	**Answer**
1	
2	
3	
4	
5	
6	
7	
8	
9	
10	
11	
12	
Number Correct:	

• ***Reviewing number facts***

1-38

Operation "Close Watch"

Think about your strategy

(for 2 players)

Equipment

Calculator
Record sheet
Pencil

"n"		"n"		"n"		"n"	
Target		**Target**		**Target**		**Target**	
Displays		**Displays**		**Displays**		**Displays**	
1		1		1		1	
2		2		2		2	
3		3		3		3	
4		4		4		4	
5		5		5		5	
6		6		6		6	
7		7		7		7	
8		8		8		8	
9		9		9		9	
10		10		10		10	
11		11		11		11	
12		12		12		12	
13		13		13		13	
14		14		14		14	
15		15		15		15	
16		16		16		16	
17		17		17		17	
18		18		18		18	
19		19		19		19	
20		20		20		20	

Instructions

1. Player A selects an "operator" number, "n" (say, 2), and writes it on the record sheet.
2. Player B picks the target number (say, 7), and writes it on the record sheet.
3. B starts, by punching in "n."
4. Take turns adding, subtracting, multiplying or dividing the number displayed by "n." (Don't erase.) Keep track of the displays on the record sheet.
5. You **win** if your move causes the target number to be displayed.
6. You **lose** if your move causes:
   - **a.** a decimal fraction to appear: or
   - **b.** an answer to be displayed that appeared earlier in the round.
7. It is a **tie** if you complete 20 turns without anyone winning.

- *Reviewing number facts*
- *Developing strategies*

Name ______________________________

1-39

Three-Button Blues

Guess how the number was made (for 2 players)

Note: You must be **very** honest to play this game!

Equipment

Calculator   Score sheet (below)   Pencil

Instructions

1. Push 3 buttons (say, [6] [+] [2]) while your partner looks the other way.
2. Push [=] and show your partner the answer (8).
   Write this "target" number in the correct space on the score sheet.
3. Keep a tally of the number of guesses (maximum: 10, 𝍸𝍸) that your partner takes to find the buttons you pushed.

   Example target: 8

Guesses		
	1 + 7	wrong
	4 × 2	wrong
	2 + 6	right (6+2=2+6)
	Score:	/// (3)

4. Trade places, so that you do the guessing.
5. After 5 rounds, total the scores made by both players.

The player with the **lowest** score wins!

	Name:			Name:		
Round	**Target**	**Tally**	**Score**	**Target**	**Tally**	**Score**
1						
2						
3						
4						
5						
	Total score:			**Total score:**		

- *Reviewing number facts*
- *Developing strategies*

Name ____________________

1-40

Dangerous Division

Challenge your division skills (for 2 to 5 players)

Equipment

Number cards (cut out and placed in a box)
Calculator
Blank cards (4 cm by 8 cm)
Pencil
Scratch paper

Instructions

1. One player picks 4 number cards from the box, without looking, and spreads them out for all to see (say, 2, 8, 6, 5).
2. All the players then have 1 min to arrange the numbers on the cards into two numerals (using paper and pencil) so that one divides evenly into the other (say, 256 ÷ 8).
3. The players write their answers on blank cards and, when all are ready, "declare" by showing their answers.
4. The players check the answers with the calculator to make sure that one number does divide evenly into the other.
5. The player who used the largest divisor wins the round (say, 56 ÷ 28).
6. Return the number cards to the box. Play continues with the next player picking 4 new cards.

1	2	3	4	5
6	7	8	9	0
1	2	3	4	5
6	7	8	9	0

Sample "Declaration" Card

256 ÷ 8

• *Reinforcing division skills*

Name ____________________________

1-41

Big Number Wins

Watch the order!

(for 2 to 4 players)

Equipment

20 number cards (cut out and put in a box)
4 operation cards (cut out)
Calculator
Score sheet (below)
Pencil

Instructions

1. Draw 5 number cards from the box without looking. Put the 5 number cards and all 4 operation cards in the order which you think will give the biggest answer. (say, $3 \times 9 + 4 \div 1 - 2$)
2. Use the calculator to find the answer. Record it on your score sheet. Return the 5 number cards to the box and mix them up.
3. The other players then take turns doing steps 1 and 2.
4. Play continues until all players have had 5 turns.
5. The player with the **highest total** wins.

1	2	3	4	5
6	7	8	9	0
1	2	3	4	5
6	7	8	9	0

+	−
×	÷

Name:	
Round 1	
Round 2	
Round 3	
Round 4	
Round 5	
Total	

Name:	
Round 1	
Round 2	
Round 3	
Round 4	
Round 5	
Total	

Name:	
Round 1	
Round 2	
Round 3	
Round 4	
Round 5	
Total	

Name:	
Round 1	
Round 2	
Round 3	
Round 4	
Round 5	
Total	

- *Understanding order of operations*
- *Using special calculator algorithms*

Name ______________________________

1-42

The Magician

Practice, then astound your friends

Equipment
Calculator
Pencil
Paper

1. Age Trick

Example: Born in November, Age 12

a.	Punch in the number of the month you were born.	11
b.	Multiply by 10.	110
c.	Add 10.	120
d.	Multiply result by 10.	1200
e.	Add your age in years.	1212
f.	Subtract 100.	1112

11 = Month you were born; 12 = Age

2. Chain Trick

		Example
a.	Pick any number.	9
b.	Add 1.	10
c.	Square your sum and record the answer.	100
d.	Now square your original number.	81
e.	Add 1 to it.	82
f.	Add result to twice original number (82+(9×2)).	100
	What happened?	
	Try again!	

• *Developing algebraic reasoning*

Beginning Calculator Math

Name ____________________

1-43

Pattern Mysteries: Part I

Predict what will happen

1. Use your calculator:

5 × 5 = ______________

5 × 55 = ______________

5 × 555 = ______________

Predict:

5 × __________ = ______________

______ × __________ = ______________

______ × __________ = ______________

Check your guesses.

2. Use your calculator:

6 × 7 = ______________

66 × 67 = ______________

666 × 667 = ______________

Predict:

______ × ______ = ______________

For X-perts!

__________ × __________ = ______________

__________ × __________ = ______________

3. Use your calculator:

1 × 8 − 1 = ______________

21 × 8 − 1 = ______________

321 × 8 − 1 = ______________

Predict:

4321 × 8 − 1 = ______________

__________ × __ − __ = ______________

__________ × __ − __ = ______________

Check your guesses.

• ***Detecting and extending patterns***

Name ________________________________

1-44

Pattern Mysteries: Part II

Look closely!

1. Use your calculator:

$1 \times 9 + 2 =$ ______

$12 \times 9 + 3 =$ ______

$123 \times 9 + 4 =$ ______

Predict:

______ $\times$ 9 + __ = ______

______ $\times$ __ + __ = ______

______ $\times$ __ + __ = ______

Check with your calculator.

2. Use your calculator:

$1 \times 9 - 1 =$ ______

$21 \times 9 - 1 =$ ______

$321 \times 9 - 1 =$ ______

Predict:

______ $\times 9 - 1 =$ ______

______ $\times 9 - 1 =$ ______

______ $\times 9 - 1 =$ ______

Check your guesses.

3. Use your calculator:

$1 \times 8 + 1 =$ 9

$12 \times 8 + 2 =$ 98

$123 \times 8 + 3 =$ ______

Predict:

______ $\times$ 8 + ____ = ______

______ $\times$ 8 + ____ = ______

______ $\times$ 8 + ____ = ______

______ $\times$ 8 + ____ = ______

Check with your calculator.

• *Detecting and extending patterns*

Beginning Calculator Math

Name ______________________

1-45

The High Cost of Crime

How much was stolen?

Mugsy stole everything on this page.
Make a list of all stolen items.
Calculate the total value of the stolen goods.

$459.00 $555.00 $178.95 $87.98 $129.00 $77.50 $34.95

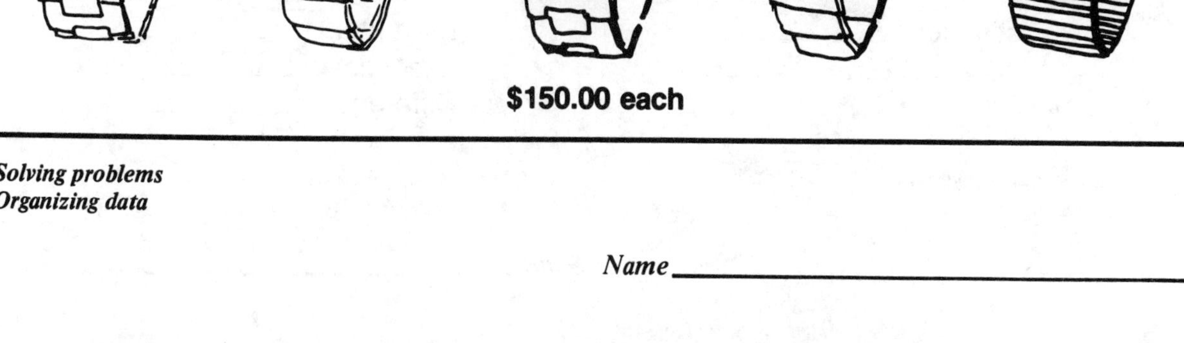

$150.00 each

• *Solving problems*
• *Organizing data*

Name ______________________

1-46

Some Costs of Living

Take an imaginary shopping trip

Write down your estimate for the cost of the articles in each circle.
Then find the exact cost with your calculator.

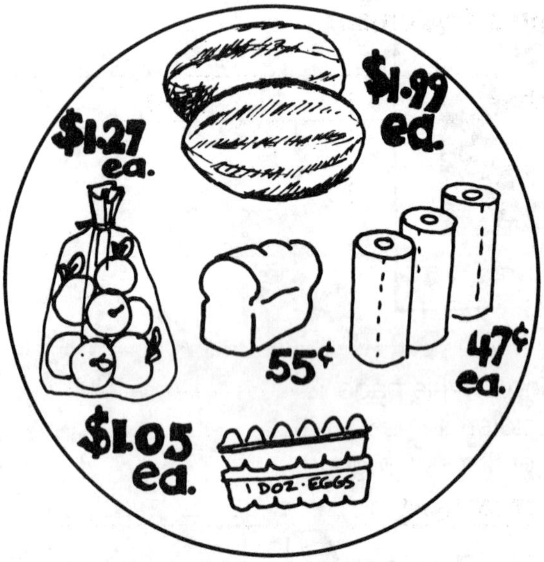

1. Estimate: ____________
Exact cost: ____________
Difference: ____________

2. Estimate: ____________
Exact cost: ____________
Difference: ____________

3. Estimate: ____________
Exact cost: ____________
Difference: ____________

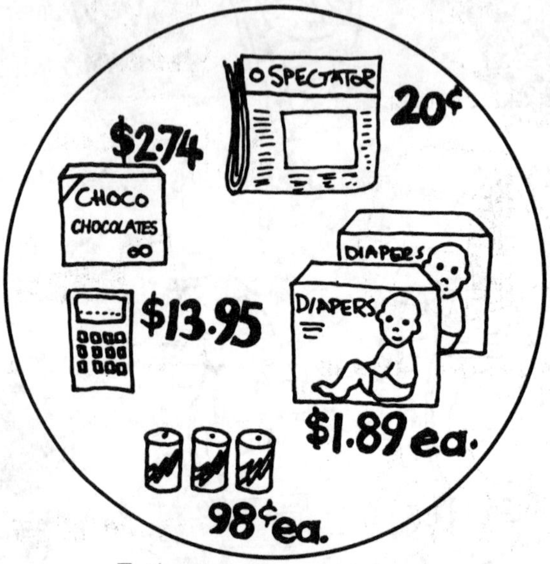

4. Estimate: ____________
Exact cost: ____________
Difference: ____________

- *Increasing consumer awareness*
- *Solving problems*

Name ______________________________

1-47

Going Camping

Add up this shopping list

List 8 items you might want to take on a 2-week camping trip.
Prepare the order form.

Order Form for Camping Equipment

Name of Item	Item Number	Cost
	Total Cost	________

P.S. You may use a sporting goods catalog to select other items not shown on this page.

Fuel (2 L can) **$2.25**
76-2216

Tent Heater **$24.95**
76-2111

Knife **$4.98**
15-1352

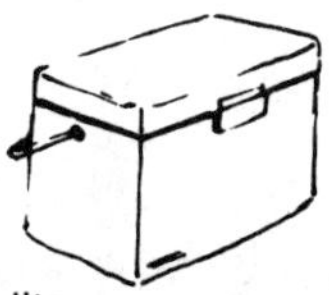

Snow-lite
Cooler Chest **$25.99**
85-4758

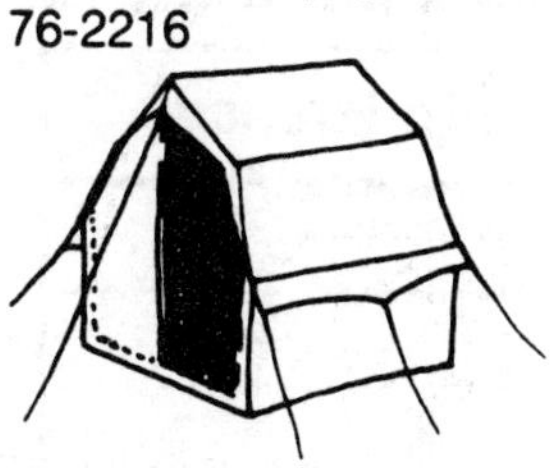

4-Person Tent **$139.95**
78-3151

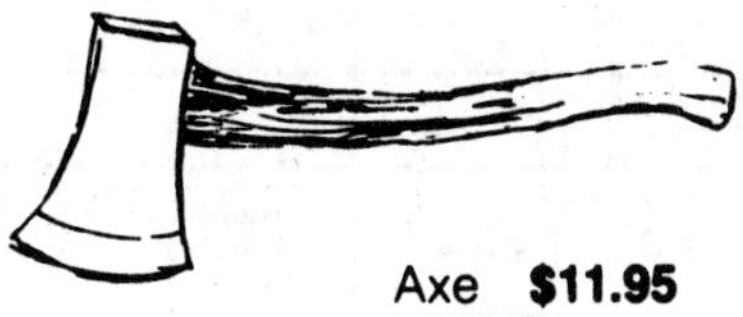

Axe **$11.95**
12-8221

Camp Cot **$11.50**
77-3333

Quality Down-Filled
Sleeping Bag **$34.95**
77-4921

Hatchet **$5.50**
12-8222

Shovel **$2.99**
16-1837

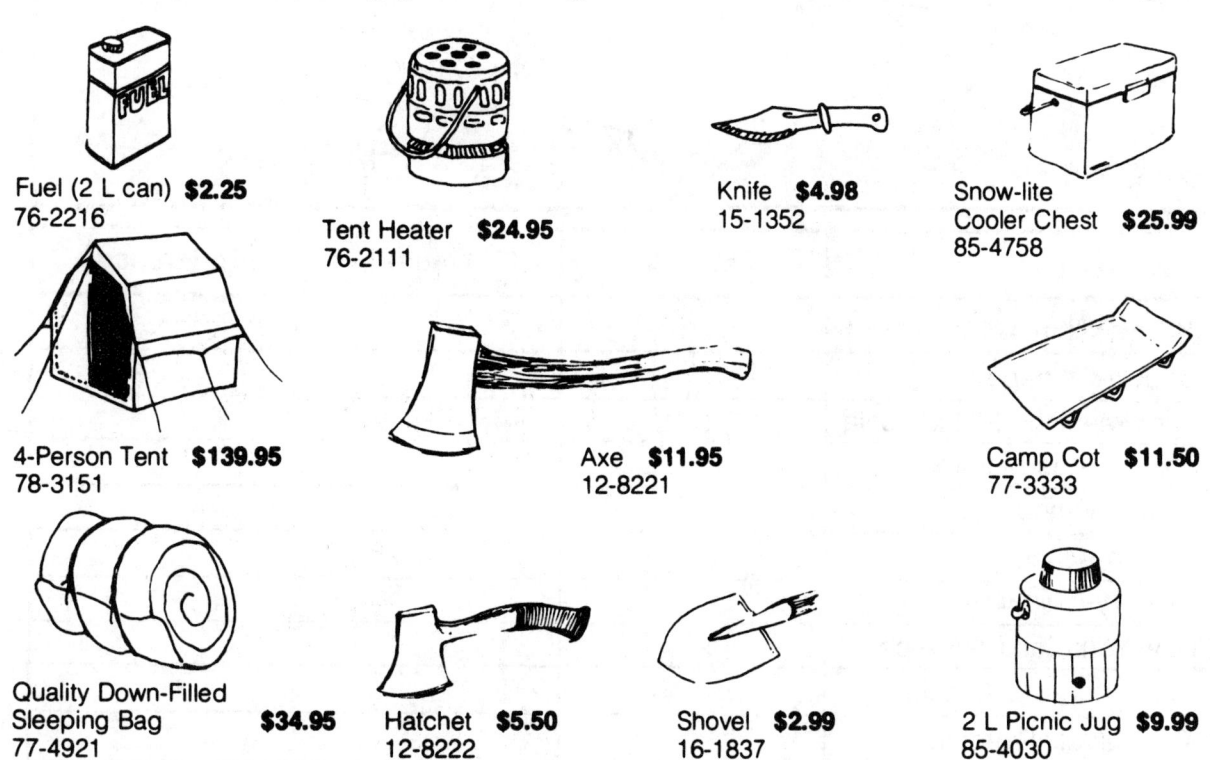

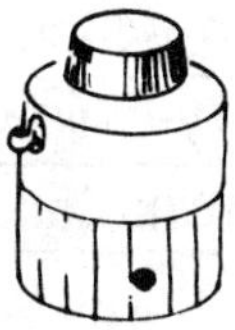

2 L Picnic Jug **$9.99**
85-4030

• ***Increasing consumer awareness***
• ***Constructing tables***

Name ______________________________

1-48

Traveling in North America

Size up some trips

Study this map of North America. Write down your estimate for the distance between the given cities. Then, find the actual distance using your calculator. Finally, record the difference between your guess and the actual distance. If your guess was 150 km too high, write +150 km; if your guess was 150 km too low, write −150 km.

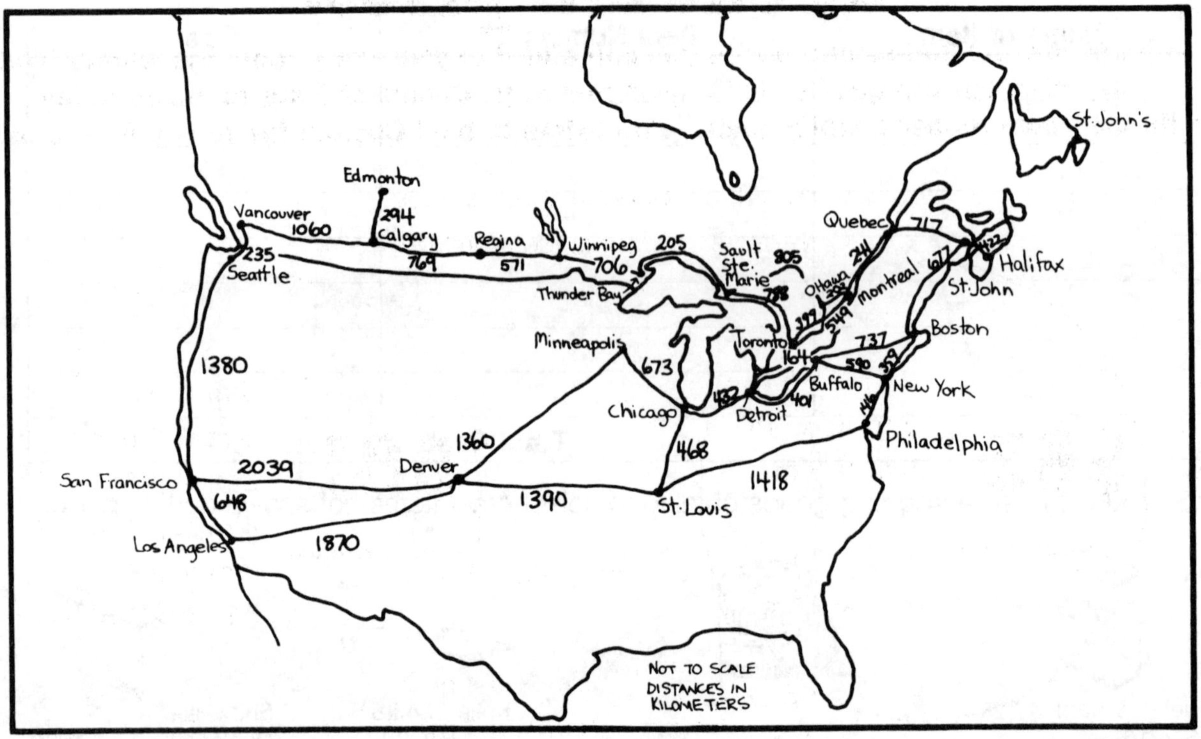

Trip	Estimate	Actual	Difference
Toronto-New York			
Ottawa-Chicago			
San Francisco-Philadelphia			
Los Angeles-Montreal			
Halifax-Vancouver			
Boston-Vancouver			
Calgary-Chicago			
New York-San Francisco			
Edmonton-Los Angeles			
Minneapolis-Toronto			

- ***Estimating in addition***
- ***Reading maps***

Name ____________________

1-49

The Great Carpet Sale

Compare the costs

up to 11 sizes at one low price!

At these low, budget-saving prices you can afford to give every room the warmth and comfort of our top quality 100% nylon pile rugs. Choice of 2 styles, ready to lay with their own rubber cushion back — no extras to buy! Custom fits to any floor area.

1. Which carpet is the best buy?

2. Which carpet is the worst buy?

$63
any size, each

- 3 m × 2.5 m
- 3 m × 2.7 m
- 3 m × 3 m
- 3 m × 3.1 m
- 4 m × 2 m
- 4 m × 2.1 m

$81
any size, each

- 3 m × 3.2 m
- 3 m × 3.6 m
- 3 m × 4 m
- 4 m × 2.4 m
- 4 m × 2.6 m
- 4 m × 2.8 m

$109
any size, each

- 3 m × 4.4 m
- 3 m × 4.6 m
- 3 m × 4.8 m
- 4 m × 3.2 m
- 4 m × 3.4 m
- 4 m × 3.6 m

$163
any size, each

- 3 m × 6.4 m
- 3 m × 6.6 m
- 3 m × 7 m
- 3 m × 7.3 m
- 4 m × 5 m
- 4 m × 5.3 m

$209
any size, each

- 3 m × 8.4 m
- 3 m × 8.7 m
- 3 m × 9 m
- 4 m × 6.7 m
- 4 m × 6.8 m
- 4 m × 7 m

- ***Increasing consumer awareness***
- ***Finding area***
- ***Finding price per unit***

Name ____________________

1-50

Painting the Shed

Find how much you'll need

1 4 L can
$2.59

2 4 L can
$2.59

3 4 L can
$4.99

4 4 L can
$4.99

5 4 L can
$5.99

6 1 L can
$0.99

7 2 L can
$1.99

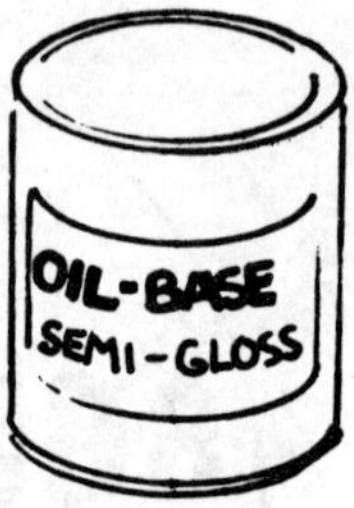

8 2 L can
$3.99

1L covers 2. 4 m²

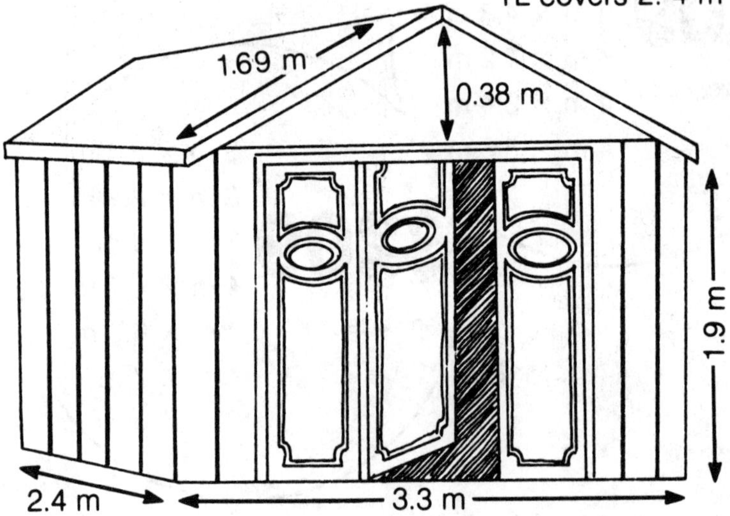

Brand	Cost of Paint for Shed
1	
2	
3	
4	
5	
6	
7	
8	

- *Finding area*
- *Developing consumer skills*

Name ____________________

1-51

MacDonald's Fence: Part I

Find the most for the least

Old MacDonald decided to fence in a rectangular piece of land for a chicken run.
Of course, he wanted to use as little fencing as possible.
If the chickens need 400 m^2, how long and how wide should the run be made?

Fill in the table:

Keep Going ↓

Area	Length	Width	Perimeter
400 m^2	1 m	400 m	802 m
400 m^2	2 m	200 m	404 m
400 m^2	4 m	100 m	
400 m^2	5 m		
400 m^2	8 m		
400 m^2	10 m		
400 m^2	15 m		

What is the most economical ratio of length to width? ________
What is a rectangle with this ratio of length to width called? ________

• ***Calculating area and ratio***

Name ______________________________

1-52

MacDonald's Fence: Part II

Keep checking until you're sure!

Now Young MacDonald remembers that a creek runs through the family farm.
Using that stream as one side of the rectangle,
she can use even less fencing and need not water the chickens anymore either.
If she still wants the run to have an area of 400 m²,
how long and how wide should she make the enclosure?

Area	Length	Width	Fencing
400 m²	1 m	400 m	801 m
400 m²	2 m	200 m	402 m
400 m²	4 m	100 m	
400 m²	5 m		
400 m²	8 m		
400 m²	10 m		
400 m²	15 m		
Keep Going →			

What do you think the ratio between length and width should be for young MacDonald's enclosure? ______

• *Calculating area and ratio*

Name ____________________

Answer Key

This section provides solutions for all sheets having exact answers. In estimation exercises, the students' approximations are more important than the exact answers, and the exact answers given here should be de-emphasized. Some sheets have no answers; these are noted in sequence in this section for easy reference.

1-1

Keys to the Calculator's Heart

Learn what those buttons do

1. Take some time to investigate the various buttons on your calculator. Don't worry about buttons marked [M] [M+] [M−] [MC] [Ex] [←→]
Find out what the C and CE buttons do. (Hint: you might have to press the CE button twice.)

2. Try these problems:

a. 3 + 2 = 5 **b.** 9 − 4 = 5 **c.** 6 × 5 = 30 **d.** 35 ÷ 7 = 5

3. Now try these:

a. 14 + 22 + 3 = 39 **b.** 4752 − 637 = 4115 **c.** 146 × 37 = 5402 **d.** 32)2752 = 86

What you may have discovered:

Keys	Function
[1] [2] [3] [4] [5] [6] [7] [8] [9] [0]	Numeral Entry
[=]	Equals
[+]	Addition
[−]	Subtraction
[×]	Multiplication
[÷]	Division
[C/CE]	Clear All/Clear Entry
[%]	Percentage
[.]	Decimal Point

Calculation Examples

Function	Example	Key Entry Sequence				Display
Addition	123 + 45.6 =	[C] [C] [1] [2] [3]	[+]	[4] [5] [.] [6]	=	168.6
Subtraction	123 − 45 =	[C] [C] [1] [2] [3]	[−]	[4] [5]	=	78
Multiplication	12 × 34 =	[C] [C] [1] [2]	[×]	[3] [4]	=	408
Division	125 ÷ 25 =	[C] [C] [1] [2] [5]	[÷]	[2] [5]	=	5

Problem 3 Answers: **a.** 39 **b.** 4115 **c.** 5402 **d.** 86

- *Introducing the calculator*

Name ____________________

1-2

The Speeding Addition Problem

Race against the clock

Find as many of the sums as you can in 3 min. The teacher will time you.
Use your calculator when necessary.

2 + 2 = 4	7 + 3 = 10	6 + 6 = 12
2 + 3 = 5	3 + 7 = 10	5 + 6 = 11
2 + 4 = 6	4 + 7 = 11	4 + 6 = 10
1 + 4 = 5	4 + 8 = 12	6 + 4 = 10
1 + 5 = 6	8 + 4 = 12	7 + 4 = 11
8 + 8 = 16	9 + 5 = 14	3 + 8 = 11
8 + 9 = 17	5 + 9 = 14	4 + 9 = 13
9 + 8 = 17	5 + 8 = 13	9 + 4 = 13
10 + 8 = 18	4 + 8 = 12	9 + 5 = 14
10 + 7 = 17	3 + 7 = 10	8 + 4 = 12
7 + 5 = 12	5 + 7 = 12	6 + 9 = 15
6 + 4 = 10	6 + 8 = 14	7 + 8 = 15
4 + 6 = 10	8 + 6 = 14	8 + 8 = 16
4 + 7 = 11	8 + 7 = 15	9 + 7 = 16
5 + 6 = 11	9 + 6 = 15	10 + 8 = 18
9 + 9 = 18	6 + 5 = 11	5 + 9 = 14
8 + 8 = 16	7 + 6 = 13	3 + 9 = 12
7 + 7 = 14	8 + 7 = 15	9 + 3 = 12
6 + 6 = 12	7 + 8 = 15	10 + 4 = 14
5 + 5 = 10	7 + 9 = 16	9 + 5 = 14

- *Learning the calculator keys*
- *Practicing addition facts*

Name ____________________

1-3

The Speeding Subtraction Problem

Review your subtraction facts

Try as many of these as you can in 3 min. The teacher will time you. Use your calculator when you need it.

7 − 2 = 5	8 − 4 = 4	13 − 5 = 8
6 − 2 = 4	10 − 4 = 6	15 − 5 = 10
6 − 3 = 3	10 − 6 = 4	15 − 10 = 5
7 − 3 = 4	12 − 6 = 6	15 − 9 = 6
7 − 4 = 3	11 − 5 = 6	15 − 7 = 8
10 − 5 = 5	16 − 6 = 10	18 − 10 = 8
12 − 5 = 7	15 − 6 = 9	19 − 10 = 9
15 − 5 = 10	15 − 9 = 6	19 − 9 = 10
15 − 6 = 9	15 − 10 = 5	18 − 9 = 9
15 − 7 = 8	14 − 9 = 5	16 − 9 = 7
16 − 7 = 9	17 − 7 = 10	16 − 8 = 8
16 − 5 = 11	16 − 7 = 9	17 − 8 = 9
18 − 5 = 13	16 − 6 = 10	16 − 7 = 9
17 − 6 = 11	15 − 7 = 8	16 − 9 = 7
18 − 6 = 12	15 − 8 = 7	15 − 10 = 5
14 − 7 = 7	8 − 0 = 8	14 − 4 = 10
15 − 6 = 9	10 − 5 = 5	14 − 10 = 4
15 − 9 = 6	12 − 2 = 10	18 − 9 = 9
14 − 9 = 5	14 − 7 = 7	17 − 7 = 10
14 − 5 = 9	16 − 6 = 10	10 − 4 = 6

- Learning the calculator keys
- Practicing subtraction facts

Name________________

1-4

The Speeding Multiplication Facts

A three-minute race

Find as many products as possible in 3 min., using your calculator when you cannot think of the answer.

0 × 3 = 0	2 × 9 = 18	7 × 4 = 28
3 × 4 = 12	3 × 9 = 27	4 × 7 = 28
4 × 3 = 12	4 × 9 = 36	5 × 7 = 35
9 × 3 = 27	9 × 4 = 36	6 × 7 = 42
9 × 2 = 18	8 × 4 = 32	6 × 6 = 36
5 × 6 = 30	4 × 8 = 32	10 × 9 = 90
6 × 5 = 30	3 × 8 = 24	9 × 9 = 81
6 × 4 = 24	8 × 3 = 24	9 × 8 = 72
7 × 4 = 28	7 × 3 = 21	8 × 9 = 72
8 × 4 = 32	7 × 2 = 14	7 × 9 = 63
9 × 7 = 63	5 × 5 = 25	7 × 8 = 56
8 × 7 = 56	6 × 5 = 30	8 × 8 = 64
7 × 8 = 56	6 × 6 = 36	8 × 7 = 56
6 × 8 = 48	7 × 6 = 42	8 × 6 = 48
5 × 8 = 40	7 × 7 = 49	5 × 6 = 30
3 × 2 = 6	5 × 6 = 30	5 × 8 = 40
7 × 6 = 42	5 × 8 = 40	3 × 6 = 18
6 × 7 = 42	8 × 8 = 64	6 × 3 = 18
7 × 7 = 49	9 × 9 = 81	8 × 6 = 48
1 × 5 = 5	8 × 2 = 16	6 × 8 = 48

- Learning the calculator keys
- Practicing multiplication facts

Name________________

1-5

The Speeding Division Facts

Another three-minute race

Do as many divisions as possible in 3 min.
Rely on your calculator when necessary.

9 ÷ 1 = 9	20 ÷ 5 = 4	70 ÷ 7 = 10
12 ÷ 3 = 4	40 ÷ 5 = 8	63 ÷ 7 = 9
12 ÷ 4 = 3	50 ÷ 5 = 10	63 ÷ 9 = 7
16 ÷ 4 = 4	60 ÷ 10 = 6	54 ÷ 9 = 6
20 ÷ 4 = 5	70 ÷ 10 = 7	27 ÷ 9 = 3
24 ÷ 8 = 3	15 ÷ 5 = 3	18 ÷ 9 = 2
24 ÷ 3 = 8	30 ÷ 5 = 6	18 ÷ 2 = 9
27 ÷ 3 = 9	30 ÷ 6 = 5	36 ÷ 4 = 9
30 ÷ 3 = 10	36 ÷ 6 = 6	72 ÷ 8 = 9
15 ÷ 3 = 5	48 ÷ 6 = 8	80 ÷ 8 = 10
80 ÷ 10 = 8	56 ÷ 8 = 7	10 ÷ 2 = 5
70 ÷ 10 = 7	28 ÷ 4 = 7	12 ÷ 2 = 6
70 ÷ 7 = 10	16 ÷ 4 = 4	24 ÷ 4 = 6
63 ÷ 7 = 9	16 ÷ 2 = 8	48 ÷ 8 = 6
56 ÷ 7 = 8	8 ÷ 2 = 4	48 ÷ 6 = 8
6 ÷ 6 = 1	14 ÷ 7 = 2	35 ÷ 5 = 7
12 ÷ 6 = 2	28 ÷ 7 = 4	40 ÷ 5 = 8
24 ÷ 6 = 4	56 ÷ 7 = 8	36 ÷ 6 = 6
48 ÷ 6 = 8	49 ÷ 7 = 7	64 ÷ 8 = 8
42 ÷ 6 = 7	35 ÷ 7 = 5	81 ÷ 9 = 9

• *Learning the calculator keys*
• *Practicing division facts*

Name ______________

1-6

The Great Mathematical Message

Accuracy will pay off

Now let's see if you can make the calculator calculate!
Try these exercises.

1. Use your answers to decode the messages.

a.

R	O	S	B	E	T	D	Y	U
1	2	3	4	5	6	7	8	9

8	8569	252
×9	− 278	× 18
72	8291	4536
DO	YOUR	BEST!

b.

E	I	C	R	T	H	M	N	K
1	2	3	4	5	6	7	8	9

1941	614,238
× 29	+101,185
56,289	715,423
THINK	METRIC!

2. Complete the 4 operations.

To check your work, compute the sum of the 4 answers.
It should be a number with all digits the same. (44,444)

a. 5843 + 4604 = 10,447 **b.** 794 × 42 = 33,348

c. 684 − 132 = 552 **d.** 1358 ÷ 14 = 97

• *Learning the calculator keys*
• *Practicing calculator operation*

Name ______________

1-7

Monster Math

Go carefully to get the picture

Join the answers, in the order given, to complete the picture.

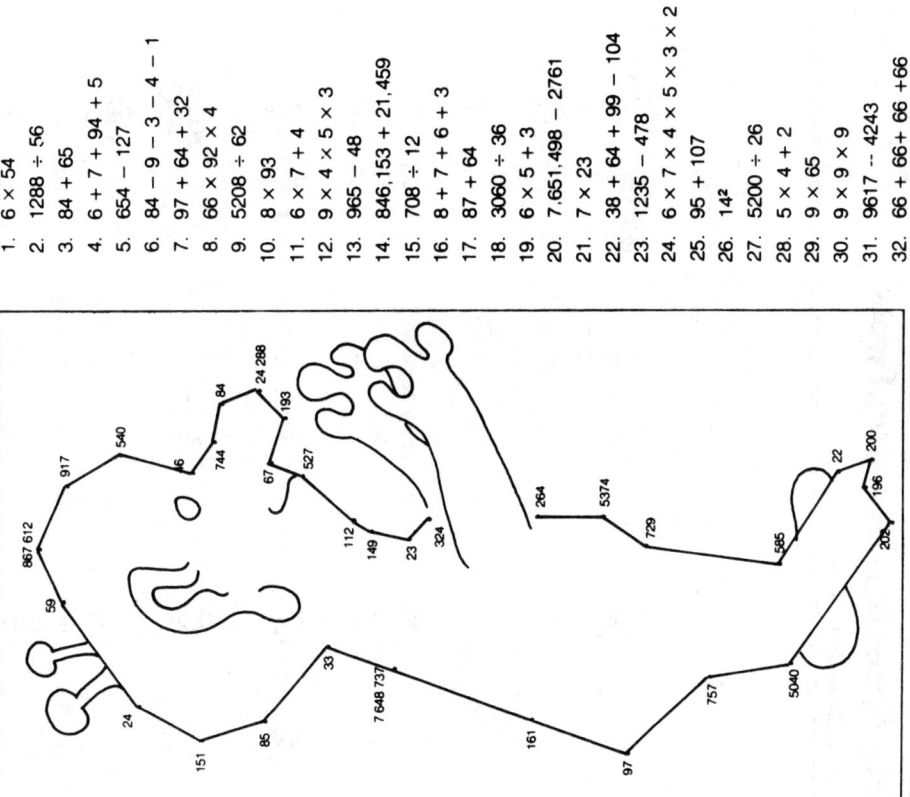

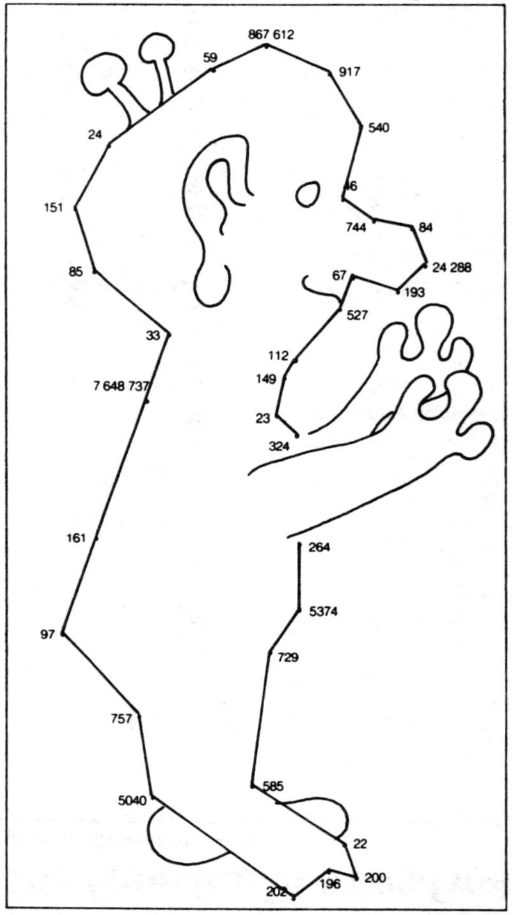

1. 6 × 54
2. 1288 ÷ 56
3. 84 + 65
4. 6 + 7 + 94 + 5
5. 654 − 127
6. 84 − 9 − 3 − 4 − 1
7. 97 + 64 + 32
8. 66 × 92 × 4
9. 5208 ÷ 62
10. 8 × 93
11. 6 × 7 + 4
12. 9 × 4 × 5 × 3
13. 965 − 48
14. 846,153 + 21,459
15. 708 ÷ 12
16. 8 + 7 + 6 + 3
17. 87 + 64
18. 3060 ÷ 36
19. 6 × 5 + 3
20. 7,651,498 − 2761
21. 7 × 23
22. 38 + 64 + 99 − 104
23. 1235 − 478
24. 6 × 7 × 4 × 5 × 3 × 2
25. 95 + 107
26. 14^2
27. 5200 ÷ 26
28. 5 × 4 + 2
29. 9 × 65
30. 9 × 9 × 9
31. 9617 -- 4243
32. 66 + 66+ 66 +66

• *Practicing calculator operation*

Name ________________

1-8

Crossnumber Puzzle

Will they all match up?

[1] 6	[13] 3			[2] 8	[14] 2
	[3] 5	[15] 2	[16] 7		6
[17] 6		[4] 5	4		
[5] 4	3		[6] 2	6	1
		[7] 6	8		
[8] 3	0	4			[18] 7
		[9] 5	[19] 3		6
[10] 4	[20] 5		7		1
	3		[11] 4	2	5
	[12] 6	4	8		

Across

1. 9 × 7
2. 37 + 25 + 20
3. 25 × 25 − 98
4. 9 × 6
5. 2881 ÷ 67
6. 87 × 3
7. 166 − 98
8. 76 × 4
9. 6 × 8 + 5
10. 44,415 ÷ 987
11. 25 × 17
12. 54 × 12

Down

7. 54 × 12 − 3
13. 7 × 5
14. 892 − 866
15. 5^2
16. 3561 + 2457 + 1410
17. 8^2
18. 1523 × 5
19. 7335 − 3587
20. 504,912 ÷ 942

• *Developing speed and accuracy*

Name ________________

1-9

Calculator versus Calculator

Can you outthink the machine?

Time yourself!

1. Do the following problems *without* using the calculator.

Starting Time: ________

4 + 8 + 2 = 14

2 × 3 × 2 = 12

20 − 10 − 4 = 6

40 ÷ 5 ÷ 2 = 4

12 × 100 = 1200

1500 ÷ 3 = 500

45 + 23 = 68

100 − 74 = 26

45 × 5 = 225

4)120 = 30

Finishing Time: ________

Time needed *without* the calculator: ________

2. Do the following problems *using* the calculator instead of your head.

Starting Time: ________

3 + 6 + 5 = 14

4 × 3 × 4 = 48

25 − 5 − 7 = 13

30 ÷ 3 ÷ 5 = 2

16 × 100 = 1600

1800 ÷ 3 = 600

52 + 34 = 86

100 − 67 = 33

62 × 6 = 372

3)150 = 50

Finishing Time: ________

Time needed *using* the calculator: ________

• *Using the calculator judiciously*

1-10

The Great Turnover

Making numbers talk

To solve this crossword puzzle, do the arithmetic questions given as clues, and then invert the calculator. The numerals on the display will look like letters, and a word will be spelled. (Disregard the decimal point in the display.) Write these words in the correct spaces, as for a regular crossword puzzle.

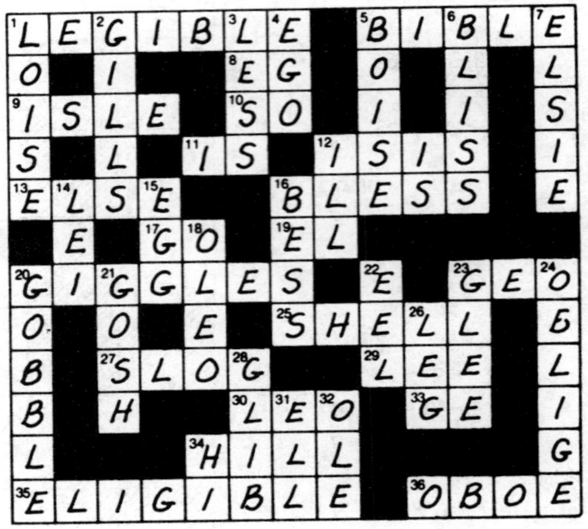

Across

1. Three million, seven hundred eighty-one thousand, nine hundred thirty-seven
5. 191 × 11 × 18
8. 9^2 + 12
9. 2542 + 1209
10. 1 ÷ 2
11. 17 × 3
12. 3 × 17 × 101
13. (400 − 3) × 9
16. 27,689 + 27,689
17. 0.3 × 3
19. 37 + 36
20. 5,380,000 − 81
23. 3 − 2.61
25. 5 × 15,469
27. 323 × 5 × 5 + 1000
29. 25 × 14 − 13
30. 1 − 0.63
33. 13 × 3
34. 2^3 × 463 + 4010
35. 300^3 + 10,819,173
36. 7 × 11 × 2 × 2 × 2 × 5

Down

1. 2589 + 6894 + 21,475 + 4149
2. 80,000 − 22,281
3. 791 × 7
4. 1 − 0.07
5. 2 × 2 × 8777
6. 90,846 − 35,668
7. 30,000 + 1000 + 500 + 70 + 3
12. 23 × 23 + 242
14. 12 × 12 − 7
15. 331 + 331 + 331
16. 17 × 9 × 9 × 2 × 2 + 30
18. 1 − 0.630
20. 378,809 × 1
21. 9 × 3 × 167
22. 500 + 130 + 103
23. 3 × 1000 + 3 × 100 + 7 × 10 + 9 × 1
24. (10,000 + 9589) × 5 × 2 × 2
26. 9 + 0.37
28. 7 × 2 × 577 + 101
31. 35 × 23 − 32
32. (5^2 + 12) × 10
34. 7 × 2

• *Working with large numbers*
• *Developing speed and accuracy*

1-11

Bigger Number Tips the Scales

Think bigger is "heavier"

Place each pair of numbers on the proper side of the balance.
The first example is done for you. Check with your calculator.

		Left side of balance	Right side of balance
60 + 50	90 + 30	60+50	90+30
53 + 72	20 + 130	53+72	20+130
109 + 72	90 + 90	90+90	109+72
901 + 716	800 + 815	800+815	901+716
384 + 376	600 + 170	384+376	600+170
232 + 537	250 + 520	232+537	250+520
118 + 420	220 + 323	118+420	220+323
624 + 193	600 + 200	600+200	624+193
722 + 484	500 + 600	500+600	722+484
819 + 193	510 + 500	510+500	819+193
489 + 215	500 + 200	500+200	489+215
758 + 176	510 + 333	510+333	758+176

- *Estimating in addition*
- *Rounding to the nearest ten*
- *Comparing sizes of numbers*

Name ____________

1-12

Which is Greater?

The nearest hundred will get you close

Insert <, =, or > to make the statements true.
The first one is done for you.

161 + 253 < 272 + 249
353 + 496 < 420 + 510
109 + 672 > 391 + 314

910 + 716 > 815 + 627
384 + 376 > 616 + 123
232 + 537 > 255 + 351

118 + 420 < 323 + 622
624 + 193 > 262 + 345
722 + 484 > 560 + 444

819 + 193 = 515 + 497
489 + 215 < 521 + 812
758 + 176 < 333 + 614

Now check with your calculator.

- *Estimating in addition*
- *Rounding to the nearest ten or hundred*
- *Comparing number values*

Name ____________

1-13

One Higher, One Lower

Estimating bigger and smaller numbers

Estimate the answer for each addition.
Circle the smallest sum in each triangle. Box the largest sum.
The first example is done for you.

Addition	Estimate	Estimate
145 + 243	150 + 240	140 + 240
857 + 348	860 + 350	860 + 340
321 + 304	320 + 300	320 + 310
637 + 555	640 + 550	640 + 560
217 + 244	210 + 240	220 + 240
104 + 568	100 + 570	100 + 560
568 + 141	570 + 140	560 + 140
384 + 374	380 + 370	380 + 380
624 + 262	625 + 260	620 + 260
537 + 132	540 + 130	530 + 130
338 + 298	330 + 300	340 + 300
595 + 263	600 + 260	590 + 265

Now check using your calculator.

- *Estimating in addition*
- *Rounding to the nearest ten*

Name ____________________

1-14

Guess the Shortest Route

The nearest ten will help

Mr. Schulz goes from school to school with his puppet show.
Next month, he will visit schools in Brick City, Dog Town, Railroad Junction, and Mass City.
Using the map below, estimate the distance traveled from Mr. Schulz's home in Beanburg
if he takes the following routes.

Estimates

1. Beanburg, Brick City, Dog Town, Railroad Junction, Mass City, Beanburg 352 km
2. Beanburg, Dog Town, Mass City, Railroad Junction, Brick City, Beanburg 423 km
3. Beanburg, Railroad Junction, Mass City, Brick City, Dog Town, Beanburg 435 km
4. Beanburg, Brick City, Railroad Junction, Mass City, Dog Town, Beanburg 423 km
5. Beanburg, Dog Town, Brick City, Railroad Junction, Mass City, Beanburg 394 km

Check the results with your calculator. Which of the 5 routes is the shortest? Route 1.

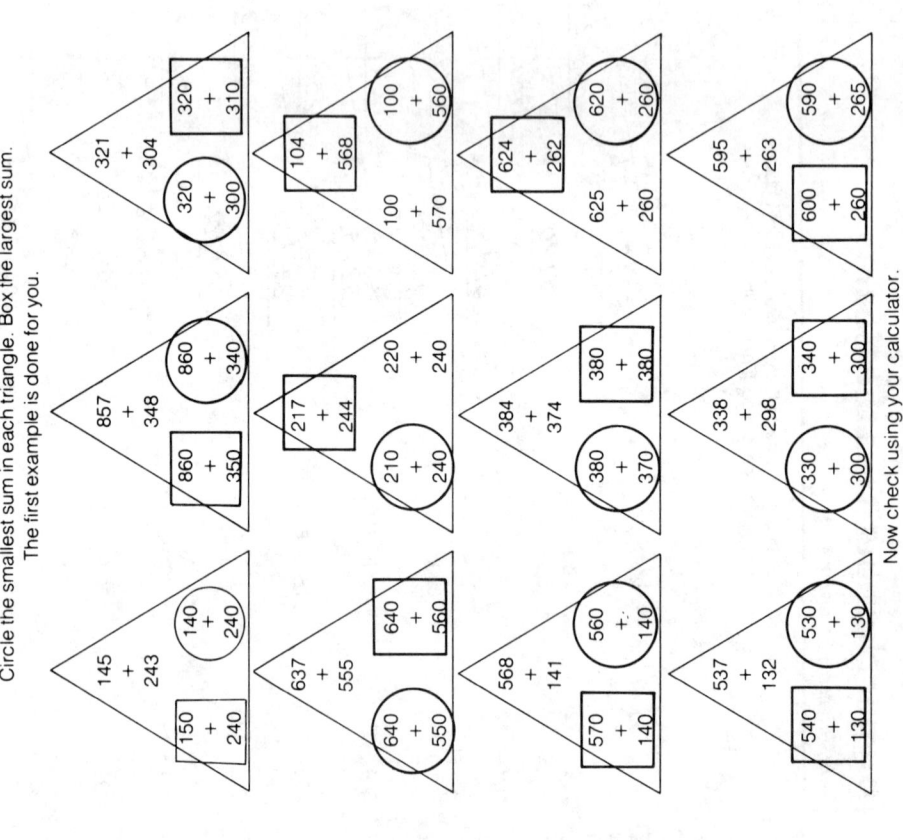

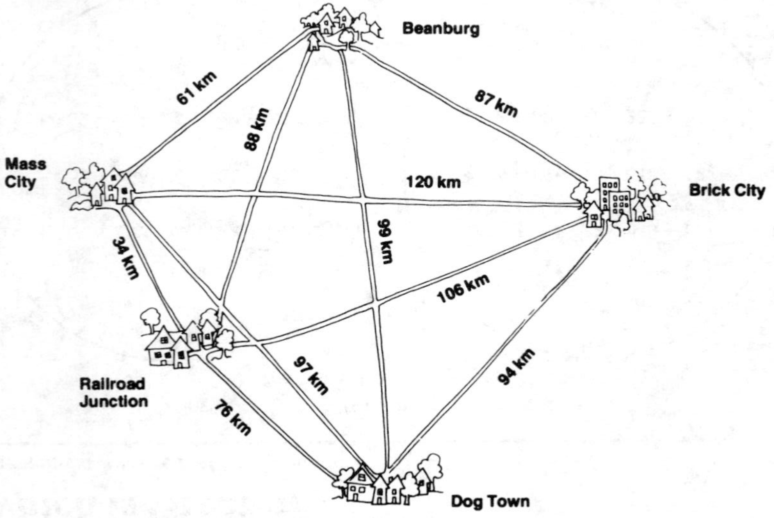

Is there a shorter route? No

- *Estimating in addition*
- *Rounding*
- *Reading maps*

Name ____________________

1-15
How Many Hundreds: Part I
Estimate, then calculate

Estimate to the nearest hundred. When you finish the page, calculate the exact answers to see how close you were.

320 +429 700	204 +127 331	389 +413 802	790 +538 1328
449 +683 1100	255 +840 1095	145 +579 724	421 +296 717
2681 +582 3300	1525 +766 2291	868 +1304 2172	4939 +873 5812
2810 +4688 7500	1599 +1001 2600	2945 +5496 8441	1615 +9584 11,199
8535 +865 9400	542 +5715 6257	3087 +756 3843	9499 +192 9691
323 355 184 9 + 34 900	10 474 54 8 +595 1141	33 91 101 192 + 64 481	109 77 63 50 + 71 370

- *Estimating in addition*
- *Rounding to the nearest hundred*
- *Adding four-digit numbers*

Name ____________________

1-16
How Many Hundreds: Part II
Rounding makes it faster

Estimate to the nearest hundred. When you finish the page, calculate the exact answers to see how close you were.

546 + 471 = About 1000 (1017)

372 + 106 = 478

211 + 934 = 1145

120 + 586 = 706

111 + 373 = 484

7898 + 7355 = About 15,000 (15,253)

4494 + 2214 = 6708

2557 + 1215 = 3772

1454 + 9506 = 10,960

8278 + 3760 = 12,038

71 + 886 = About 1000 (957)

409 + 696 = 1105

232 + 38 = 270

32 + 645 = 677

753 + 650 = 1403

4710 + 229 = About 4900 (4939)

867 + 6263 = 7130

4936 + 6193 = 11,129

280 + 8837 = 9117

1598 + 817 = 2415

15 + 98 + 7 + 90 + 32 + 7 + 5 + 2 + 27 = About 300 (283)

517 + 38 + 9 + 5 + 953 + 3 + 29 + 7 = 1561

54 + 22 + 565 + 7 + 5 + 3 + 85 + 33 = 774

17 + 554 + 491 + 998 + 83 + 4 + 11 = 2158

568 + 319 + 30 + 32 + 3362 + 24 + 104 = 4439

- *Estimating in addition*
- *Rounding to the nearest hundred*
- *Adding four-digit numbers*

Name ____________________

Estimation

1-17

About the Same

Think rounding to tens

Join a subtraction phrase from the left-hand column to one that will have approximately the same answer in the right-hand column.
Circle the one you think has the larger answer.
An example has been done for you.

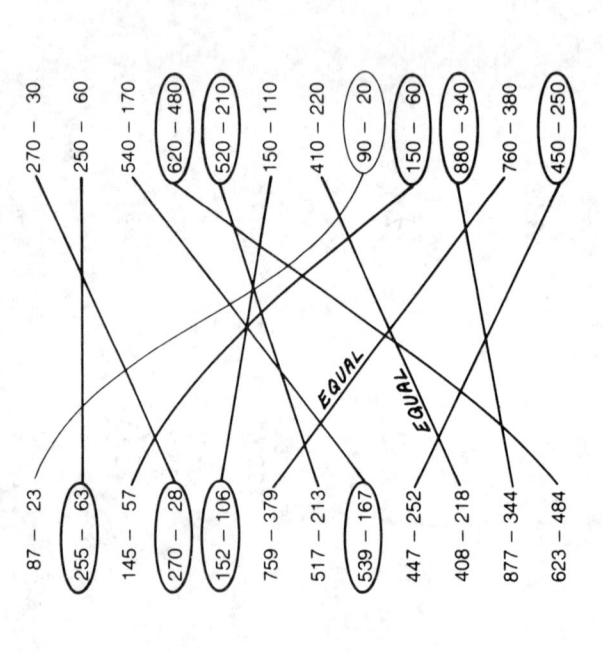

87 – 23	270 – 30
(255 – 63)	250 – 60
145 – 57	540 – 170
(270 – 28)	(620 – 480)
(152 – 106)	(520 – 210)
759 – 379	150 – 110
517 – 213	410 – 220
(539 – 167)	(90 – 20)
447 – 252	(150 – 60)
408 – 218	(880 – 340)
877 – 344	760 – 380
623 – 484	(450 – 250)

EQUAL

EQUAL

Check with your calculator.

- *Estimating in subtraction*
- *Rounding to the nearest ten*
- *Subtracting three-digit numbers*

Name ______________________________

Estimation

1-18

Speedy Subtraction: Part I

Think in tens and hundreds

Write down your estimates.

653 − 47 = 606 (Think 650 − 50 = 600)	104 − 68 = 36 (Think 100 − 70)	595 − 63 = 532	338 − 90 = 248
819 − 192 = 627	716 − 109 = 607	624 − 262 = 362	355 − 193 = 162
6542 − 671 = 5871	6484 − 3722 = 2762	2118 − 1120 = 998	1205 − 163 = 1042
6857 − 1348 = 5509	5716 − 3901 = 1815	9915 − 221 = 9694	9094 − 4089 = 5005
890 − 40 = 850	6112 − 2326 = 3786	132 − 37 = 95	75,321 − 304 = 75,017
563 − 428 = 135	24,384 − 374 = 24,010	916 − 44 = 872	2555 − 637 = 1918

Now check your estimates using the calculator.

- *Estimating in subtraction*
- *Rounding to the nearest ten or hundred*

Name ______________________________

1-19

Speedy Subtraction: Part II

Look for the tens

Write down your estimates.

255 − 63 = About 200 (192)	152 − 99 = About 50 (53)
145 − 41 = 104	280 − 106 = 174
827 − 57 = 770	759 − 243 = 516
470 − 49 = 421	908 − 879 = 29
267 − 26 = 241	886 − 517 = 369
294 − 213 = About 80 (81)	798 − 56 = About 740 (742)
401 − 167 = 234	323 − 17 = 306
539 − 308 = 231	879 − 183 = 696
447 − 175 = 272	104 − 62 = 42
998 − 259 = 739	8707 − 33 = 8674

338 − 19 − 71 − 76 − 8 − 109 = About 60 (55)

623 − 90 − 53 − 35 − 198 − 4 = 243

201 − 98 − 36 − 11 − 49 − 7 = 0

822 − 2 − 168 − 81 − 1 − 204 = 366

685 − 31 − 53 − 7 − 3 − 99 = 492

Now check your estimates using the calculator.

- *Estimating in subtraction*
- *Rounding to the nearest ten or hundred*

Name ______________________

1-20

Find the Smaller Number

Watch for those small differences

Put an X next to the subtraction sentence (A or B) which will give the smallest answer.
Put an X in both columns if the two answers are the same.
Do not work out the differences. Instead, carefully compare the sentences.
You may check your guesses with the calculator.

A	X	B	X
685 − 299		680 − 299	X
502 − 159		502 − 160	X
847 − 274	X	850 − 274	
668 − 320	X	670 − 322	X
320 − 232	X	320 − 230	
447 − 111	X	450 − 111	
784 − 310		780 − 310	X
550 − 300	X	550 − 295	
680 − 300	X	685 − 300	
847 − 270	X	850 − 270	
950 − 480	X	951 − 477	
822 − 510		822 − 513	X

A	X	B	X
670 − 320	X	668 − 322	
447 − 110		450 − 110	X
846 − 470		850 − 468	X
554 − 300		554 − 295	X
480 − 240	X	479 − 244	
324 − 232		324 − 230	X
950 − 477	X	951 − 480	
780 − 308		784 − 308	X
850 − 470	X	846 − 468	
820 − 510	X	820 − 513	
479 − 240	X	480 − 244	
500 − 159		500 − 160	X

- *Estimating in subtraction*
- *Comparing subtraction sentences*
- *Adjusting for rounding error*

Name ______________________

1-21

Round and Multiply

Think with tens again

Circle the best estimate. Check with your calculator.

Think: 70 × 4 = 280 Which estimate is closest?

Product	Estimates		
73 × 4	250	**300**	350
92 × 5	400	**450**	500
81 × 7	**600**	700	800
29 × 5	**150**	200	250
54 × 6	200	250	**300**
66 × 4	**250**	300	350
79 × 8	600	**650**	700
49 × 7	**350**	400	450
95 × 6	500	**550**	600
38 × 9	**350**	375	400
56 × 3	150	**175**	200
67 × 8	450	500	**550**

- Estimating in multiplication
- Rounding to the nearest ten
- Multiplying rounded numbers

Name ______________________

1-22

Easy Multiplication

Think rounding first

Record your estimate first, then calculate.

Estimates may vary

62 × 3 = 186 (Think: 60 × 3 (180))	35 × 4 = 140 (Think: 40 × 4 (160))	18 × 6 = 108 (______)	93 × 7 = 651 (______)
104 × 6 = 624 (______)	594 × 7 = 4158 (______)	338 × 5 = 1690 (______)	623 × 8 = 4984 (______)
32 × 29 = 928 (______)	18 × 37 = 666 (______)	42 × 35 = 1470 (______)	84 × 63 = 5292 (______)
429 × 35 = 15,015 (______)	114 × 85 = 9690 (______)	653 × 57 = 37,221 (______)	371 × 93 = 34,503 (______)
684 × 91 = 62,244 (______)	389 × 70 = 27,230 (______)	221 × 73 = 16,133 (______)	126 × 16 = 2016 (______)

Now check your estimates on the calculator.

- Estimating in multiplication
- Rounding to the nearest ten or hundred

Name ______________________

1-23

Guess One Higher, One Lower

Choose your challenge well

Write down your estimate for the range into which the product will fall.
Make the range as small as you dare.
Check by finding the exact product (P) with your calculator.

Step 1
Step 2

	P > ?	Exact Product (P)	P < ?
94 × 6	540	564	600
53 × 7		371	
61 × 8		488	
89 × 5		445	
83 × 9		747	
74 × 3		222	
49 × 4		196	
83 × 5		415	
7 × 49		343	
6 × 37		222	
8 × 21		168	
6 × 94		564	
7 × 83		581	
5 × 42		210	
9 × 63		567	
4 × 91		364	

• *Estimating in multiplication*
• *Rounding to the nearest ten*

Name ____________________________

Sheet 1-24

Answers read "One correct keep going perfect."

1-25
Number Line Puzzle

Find the message on the line

Estimate the products. Put the corresponding letter in the correct place on the number line. If arranged correctly, the letters will spell a sentence. The first example is done for you. (Be careful! Sometimes you will have 2 letters in the same range.)

Letter	Product	
O	91 × 60	= 5460
K	58 × 70	= 4060
S	59 × 80	= 4720
I	89 × 50	= 4450
T	83 × 90	= 7470
L	74 × 30	= 2220
A	49 × 40	= 1960
E	81 × 81	= 6561
R	79 × 78	= 6162
R	60 × 95	= 5700
L	70 × 37	= 2590
R	40 × 96	= 3840
O	50 × 74	= 3700
C	90 × 57	= 5130
C	90 × 75	= 6750
W	52 × 62	= 3224

A L L W O R K I S C O R R E C T

1500 2000 2500 3000 3500 4000 4500 5000 5500 6000 6500 7000 7500

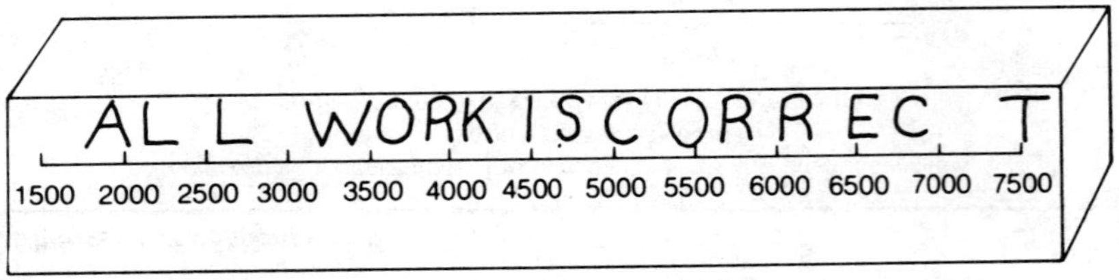

If necessary, check your estimates with your calculator.

- *Estimating in multiplication*
- *Adjusting for rounding error*
- *Using a number line*

Name _____

Estimation

Sheet 1-26

Answer words read "You are very clever."

76 *Beginning CALCULATOR MATH*

1-27

Whiz Quiz

How fast, how close?

Write your estimates.

1.

81 × 6 =	Think 80×6=480
53 × 9 =	477
31 × 7 =	217
48 × 5 =	240
87 × 8 =	696

2.

20 × 51 =	1020
28 × 88 =	2200
41 × 96 =	3936
97 × 46 =	4462
65 × 23 =	1495

3.

333 × 597 =	198,801
420 × 874 =	367,080
530 × 983 =	520,990
845 × 160 =	135,200
106 × 627 =	66,462

4.

508 × 7 =	3556
641 × 8 =	5128
809 × 6 =	4854
128 × 9 =	1152
626 × 5 =	3130

5.

827 × 27 =	22,329
131 × 76 =	9956
166 × 61 =	10,126
209 × 58 =	12,122
644 × 26 =	16,744

6.

1346 × 8 =	10,768
2015 × 8 =	16,120
1946 × 3 =	5838
4901 × 90 =	441,090
2855 × 70 =	199,850

Now check your estimates with the calculator.

- *Estimating in multiplication*
- *Rounding to the nearest ten or hundred*

Name ____________________

1-28

Quick Parts

What's about half or a third?

Find approximately $\frac{1}{2}$ of the given values. An example is done for you.

823 →	400 (411.5)
616 →	308
187 →	93.5
1375 →	687.5
779 →	389.5

Find approximately $\frac{1}{3}$ of the given values. An example is done for you.

311 →	100 (104)
589 →	196
277 →	92
688 →	229
897 →	299

Find approximately $\frac{1}{4}$ of the following numbers. An example is done for you.

523 →	125 (131)
920 →	230
643 →	161
162 →	40
369 →	92

$\frac{1}{3}$ of 313 is approximately:	104
$\frac{1}{4}$ of 554 is approximately:	138
$\frac{1}{2}$ of 233 is approximately:	116
$\frac{1}{4}$ of 981 is approximately:	245
$\frac{1}{2}$ of 506 is approximately:	253
$\frac{1}{3}$ of 624 is approximately:	208
$\frac{2}{3}$ of 173 is approximately:	115
$\frac{1}{2}$ of 726 is approximately:	363
$\frac{1}{4}$ of 266 is approximately:	66
$\frac{3}{4}$ of 307 is approximately:	230
$\frac{1}{3}$ of 496 is approximately:	165
$\frac{1}{2}$ of 544 is approximately:	272
$\frac{2}{3}$ of 267 is approximately:	178
$\frac{3}{4}$ of 806 is approximately:	604
$\frac{1}{4}$ of 963 is approximately:	241
$\frac{1}{3}$ of 354 is approximately:	118

- *Estimating fractional parts*

Name ____________________

1-29

The Educated Guess: Part I

Decide if it's really more or less

Write your estimate and indicate by + or − whether you expect the quotient to be greater than (+) or less than (−) the estimate. Then use your calculator to determine the quotient, and record it (to the nearest whole number) in the chart. Time: 6 min.

	Estimate	Quotient
695 ÷ 7	100-	99
323 ÷ 6	50+	54
388 ÷ 3		129
124 ÷ 2		62
151 ÷ 4		38
889 ÷ 9		99
554 ÷ 9		62
838 ÷ 2		419
522 ÷ 3		174
326 ÷ 7		47
191 ÷ 4		48
119 ÷ 9		13
745 ÷ 8		93
465 ÷ 4		116
703 ÷ 7		100
413 ÷ 7		59
257 ÷ 6		43
160 ÷ 3		53
100 ÷ 8		12
625 ÷ 6		104

	Estimate	Quotient
943 ÷ 2		471
158 ÷ 9		18
366 ÷ 5		73
228 ÷ 5		46
142 ÷ 4		36
203 ÷ 3		68
126 ÷ 8		16
790 ÷ 6		132
493 ÷ 4		123
307 ÷ 8		38
438 ÷ 4		109
273 ÷ 6		46
170 ÷ 4		42
106 ÷ 8		13
663 ÷ 5		132
390 ÷ 3		130
589 ÷ 4		147
367 ÷ 4		92
229 ÷ 6		38
143 ÷ 3		48

• *Estimating in division*

Name ____________________

1-30

The Educated Guess: Part II

Judge the error in your estimates

Write your estimate and indicate whether you expect the exact answer to be greater than or less than the estimate.

	Estimate	Quotient
606 ÷ 2	300+	303
34.4 ÷ 4		8.6
195 ÷ 5		39
11 ÷ 5		2.2
62.9 ÷ 7		8.99
3.84 ÷ 6		0.64
21.8 ÷ 8		2.725
123 ÷ 3		41
70.3 ÷ 7		10.04
399 ÷ 2		199.5
244 ÷ 5		48.8
13.8 ÷ 6		2.3
7.86 ÷ 5		1.572
44.6 ÷ 3		14.87
253 ÷ 7		36.14
2.95 ÷ 7		0.42
787 ÷ 4		196.75
20.9 ÷ 8		2.6125
39.4 ÷ 7		5.63
104 ÷ 4		26

	Estimate	Quotient
65.3 ÷ 5		13.06
370 ÷ 3		123.3
21 ÷ 5		4.2
119 ÷ 4		29.75
677 ÷ 9		75.22
414 ÷ 5		82.8
23.5 ÷ 3		7.83
13.3 ÷ 4		3.325
75.7 ÷ 6		12.617
430 ÷ 6		71.67
26.2 ÷ 9		2.91
14.9 ÷ 2		7.45
84.7 ÷ 3		28.23
12.7 ÷ 8		1.5875
154 ÷ 9		17.11
278 ÷ 6		46.33
74.1 ÷ 2		37.05
197 ÷ 4		49.25
5.24 ÷ 3		1.747
13.9 ÷ 9		1.54

• *Estimating in division*

Name ____________________

Estimation

1-31

The Line-Up

Visualize your answer on the line

Write the letter for each division problem in its proper place on the number line.
The first one is done for you.

1.

a.	435 ÷ 6	**e.**	429 ÷ 12
b.	74.1 ÷ 9	**f.**	760 ÷ 7
c.	627 ÷ 7	**g.**	325 ÷ 15
d.	123 ÷ 2	**h.**	81.5 ÷ 5

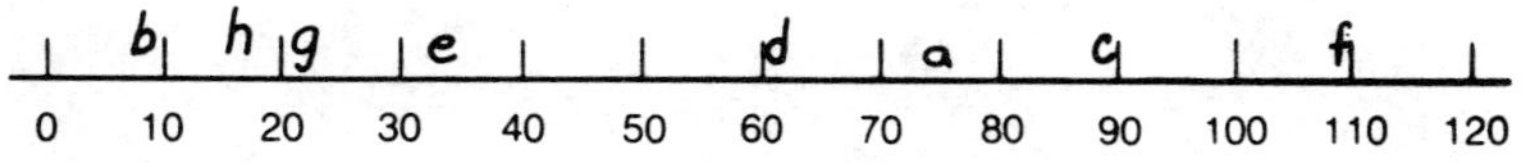

2.

a.	274 ÷ 13	**e.**	346 ÷ 6
b.	791 ÷ 8	**f.**	262 ÷ 3
c.	23.5 ÷ 17	**g.**	190 ÷ 1.8
d.	961 ÷ 30	**h.**	275 ÷ 4

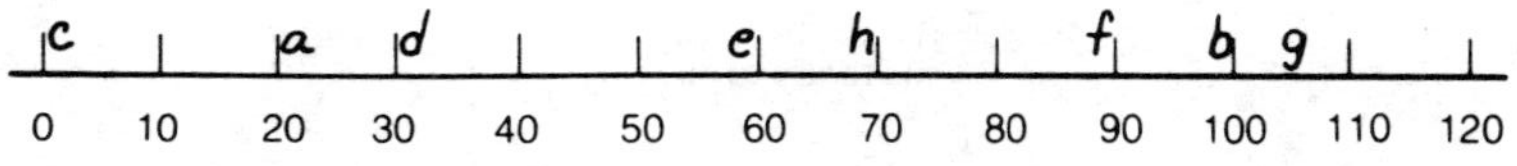

3.

a.	210 ÷ 6	**e.**	46.2 ÷ 79
b.	967 ÷ 9	**f.**	266 ÷ 12
c.	443 ÷ 8	**g.**	896 ÷ 20
d.	128 ÷ 8.1	**h.**	598 ÷ 6.7

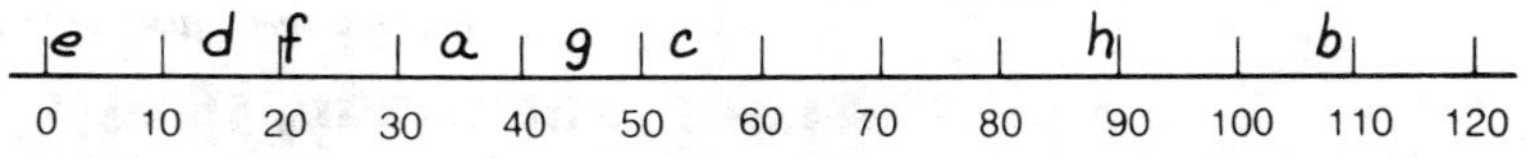

- *Estimating in division*
- *Rounding to the nearest whole number*

Name ______________________________ *41*

Sheet 1-32 through Sheet 1-42

No specific answers.

1-43

Pattern Mysteries: Part I

Predict what will happen

1. Use your calculator:

5 × 5 = 25

5 × 55 = 275

5 × 555 = 2775

Predict:

5 × 5555 = 27,775

5 × 55,555 = 277,775

5 × 555,555 = 2,777,775

Check your guesses.

2. Use your calculator:

6 × 7 = 42

66 × 67 = 4422

666 × 667 = 444,222

Predict:

6666 × 6667 = 44,442,222

For X-perts!

66,666 × 66,667 = 4,444,422,222

666,666 × 666,667 = 444,444,222,222

3. Use your calculator:

1 × 8 − 1 = 7

21 × 8 − 1 = 167

321 × 8 − 1 = 2567

Predict:

4321 × 8 − 1 = 34,567

54,321 × 8 − 1 = 434,567

654,321 × 8 − 1 = 5,234,567

Check your guesses.

• *Detecting and extending patterns*

Name ____________

1-44

Pattern Mysteries: Part II

Look closely!

1. Use your calculator:

1 × 9 + 2 = 11

12 × 9 + 3 = 111

123 × 9 + 4 = 1111

Predict:

1234 × 9 + 5 = 11,111

12,345 × 9 + 6 = 111,111

123,456 × 9 + 7 = 1,111,111

Check with your calculator.

2. Use your calculator:

1 × 9 − 1 = 8

21 × 9 − 1 = 188

321 × 9 − 1 = 2888

Predict:

4321 × 9 − 1 = 38,888

54,321 × 9 − 1 = 488,888

654,321 × 9 − 1 = 5,888,888

Check your guesses.

3. Use your calculator:

1 × 8 + 1 = 9

12 × 8 + 2 = 98

123 × 8 + 3 = 987

Predict:

1234 × 8 + 4 = 9876

12,345 × 8 + 5 = 98,765

123,456 × 8 + 6 = 987,654

1,234,567 × 8 + 7 = 9,876,543

Check with your calculator.

• *Detecting and extending patterns*

Name ____________

Sheet 1-45

Mugsy stole a total of $2272.38.

Sheet 1-46

Group 1 exact cost is $9.31. Group 2 exact cost is $18.20.
Group 3 exact cost is $10.17. Group 4 exact cost is $23.61.

Sheet 1-47

Answers will vary.

Sheet 1-48

Answers will vary. Students can list stopovers for easier checking.

1-49

The Great Carpet Sale

Compare the costs

up to 11 sizes at one low price!

At these low, budget-saving prices you can afford to give every room the warmth and comfort of our top quality 100% nylon pile rugs. Choice of 2 styles, ready to lay with their own rubber cushion back — no extras to buy! Custom fits to any floor area.

1. Which carpet is the best buy?
2. Which carpet is the worst buy?

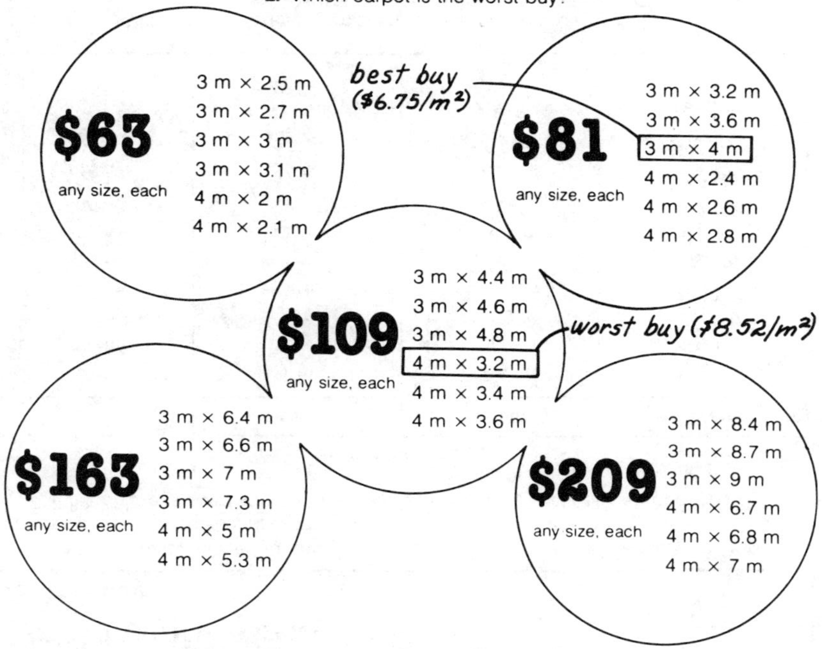

- *Increasing consumer awareness*
- *Finding area*
- *Finding price per unit*

Name ____________________

1-50

Painting the Shed

Find how much you'll need

1 4 L can **$2.59**
2 4 L can **$2.59**
3 4 L can **$4.99**
4 4 L can **$4.99**
5 4 L can **$5.99**
6 1 L can **$0.99**
7 2 L can **$1.99**
8 2 L can **$3.99**

Area of shed: without roof: 22.914 m²; including roof: 31.026 m²
Paint needed: without roof: 16.37 L → 17 L → 5 4-L cans or 9 2-L cans
including roof: 22.16 L → 23 L → 6 4-L cans or 12 2-L cans

1L covers 2. 4 m²

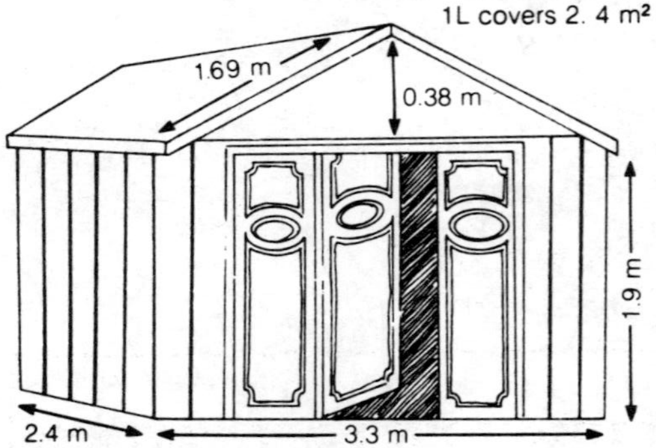

Brand	Cost of Paint for Shed (*without roof*)	(*including roof*)
1	*$12.95*	*$15.54*
2	*$12.95*	*$15.54*
3	*$24.95*	*$29.94*
4	*$24.95*	*$29.94*
5	*$29.95*	*$35.94*
6	*$16.83*	*$22.77*
7	*$17.91*	*$23.88*
8	*$35.91*	*$47.88*

- *Finding area*
- *Developing consumer skills*

Name ____________________

1-51

MacDonald's Fence: Part I

Find the most for the least

Old MacDonald decided to fence in a rectangular piece of land for a chicken run.
Of course, he wanted to use as little fencing as possible.
If the chickens need 400 m², how long and how wide should the run be made?

Fill in the table:

Area	Length	Width	Perimeter
400 m²	1 m	400 m	802 m
400 m²	2 m	200 m	404 m
400 m²	4 m	100 m	*208 m*
400 m²	5 m	*80 m*	*170 m*
400 m²	8 m	*50 m*	*116 m*
400 m²	10 m	*40 m*	*100 m*
400 m²	15 m	*26.7 m*	*83.4 m*
400 m²	*20 m*	*20 m*	*80 m*
400 m²	*25 m*	*16 m*	*82 m*
400 m²	*30 m*	*13.3 m*	*86.6 m*

Keep Going →

What is the most economical ratio of length to width? *1:1*
What is a rectangle with this ratio of length to width called? *a square*

- *Calculating area and ratio*

Name ____________________

1-52

MacDonald's Fence: Part II

Keep checking until you're sure!

Now Young MacDonald remembers that a creek runs through the family farm.
Using that stream as one side of the rectangle,
she can use even less fencing and need not water the chickens anymore either.
If she still wants the run to have an area of 400 m².
how long and how wide should she make the enclosure?

Keep Going →

Area	Length	Width	Fencing
400 m²	1 m	400 m	801 m
400 m²	2 m	200 m	402 m
400 m²	4 m	100 m	204m
400 m²	5 m	80m	165m
400 m²	8 m	50m	108m
400 m²	10 m	40m	90m
400 m²	15 m	26.7m	68.4m
400m²	20m	20m	60m
400m²	25m	16m	57m
400m²	30m	13.3m	56.6m
400m²	31m	12.9m	56.8m
400m²	29m	13.7m	56.4m
400m²	28m	14.3m	56.6m
400m²	27m	14.8m	56.6m

What do you think the ratio between length and width should be for young MacDonald's enclosure? 2:1

• *Calculating area and ratio*

Name ______________________

Teacher's Notes